# Using ICT in Primary Mathematics

## Practice and Possibilities

by

**Bob Fox**
**Ann Montague-Smith**
**and Sarah Wilkes**

**David Fulton Publishers**
London

David Fulton Publishers Ltd
Ormond House, 26–27 Boswell Street, London WC1N 3JD

First published in Great Britain by David Fulton Publishers 2000

Note: The rights of Bob Fox, Ann Montague-Smith and Sarah Wilkes to be identified as the authors of this work have been asserted by them in accordance with the Copyright, Designs and Patents Act 1988.

Copyright © Bob Fox, Ann Montague-Smith and Sarah Wilkes 2000

British Library Cataloguing in Publication Data
A catalogue record for this book is available from the British Library

ISBN 1–85346–647–6

Typeset by Elite Typesetting Techniques, Eastleigh, Hampshire
Printed in Great Britain by The Cromwell Press Ltd, Trowbridge, Wilts.

# Contents

# Acknowledgements and notes about the authors

Our thanks go to the staff and children of the schools who so kindly allowed us to work with them, to observe their practice, and who answered our endless questions. Thanks go to David Montague-Smith, who took the photographs, and Fiona Thompson, who kindly provided cartoon illustrations for this book. Our thanks also go to University College Worcester, without whose support this book could not have been written. And finally, and most importantly of all, our thanks go to our long-suffering families who were so understanding of the amount of time that it took to write this book.

Bob Fox, Ann Montague-Smith and Sarah Wilkes
Worcester, January 2000

**Bob Fox.** Bob is Senior Lecturer in Primary Education and Leader of Primary Information Communications Technology at University College Worcester, teaching both PGCE students and undergraduates training to be teachers. He was previously headteacher of a rural primary school, then an advisory teacher for IT. He is the review editor for MAPE publications.

**Ann Montague-Smith.** Ann is Principal Lecturer in Primary Education and Leader of Primary Mathematics at University College Worcester. She teaches mathematics courses for PGCE, undergraduate and in-service teachers. Previously she was a head teacher. She is an experienced writer, having written both academic books and materials for teachers and pupils.

**Sarah Wilkes.** Sarah is Senior Lecturer in Primary Education and is a member of both the ICT and Mathematics teams at University College Worcester. Previously she taught in a large, urban primary school, where she was coordinator for ICT.

# Introduction

We have written this book, using our combined first-hand experiences as class teachers, in the advisory service, and now as teacher trainers, to help teachers and students in training to consider some of the issues that surround the use of Information and Communications Technology (ICT) in today's and tomorrow's classrooms.

Of all the initiatives imposed by government upon teachers, the National Numeracy Strategy is the most radical, in that it requires fundamental changes in teaching and learning styles. No longer is the child a passive recipient of knowledge, from either their teacher or from books; instead both teacher and children are active throughout the daily mathematics lesson, with demonstration, exploration of new material and whole class discussion a major thrust in improving the quality of both teaching and learning.

At the same time as the National Numeracy Strategy is being promulgated, the importance of ICT in schools is being increased, both by the provision of extra government-funded facilities, for example through the NGfL, and through substantially increased demands made on teachers' ICT competencies.

All of this leads us to a paradox: the daily mathematics lesson, which involves whole-class, interactive teaching and dialogue between the participants, seems to preclude the use of ICT as we have known it in recent years. The National Numeracy Strategy requires that drill and practice software should not be used as a solitary activity by pupils during the mathematics lesson, unless a child has very specific, stated, special needs.

Within this book we explore the uses of ICT in mathematics teaching and learning, past and present, and we provide a rationale for its use within and beyond the daily mathematics lesson, and suggest some innovative ways forward. We do not attempt to identify specific applications for topics within the National Numeracy Strategy. Instead, we offer points for consideration to assist teachers and student teachers to make wise decisions about the appropriate use of ICT in mathematics teaching and learning, whether as part of a whole-class interactive activity, a group activity, or outside the lesson. We have reviewed some software and applications, and have included some case study material to exemplify today's and tomorrow's practice in primary schools.

Readers of the book can use it in a number of ways. It can, of course, be read from cover to cover: the contents list has been written to help the reader to identify useful material, and there is a detailed index so that the reader can dip into topics of interest. There are also sections in the book which would be useful for generating discussions in staff meetings, lectures and in-service courses.

We trust that readers will find the tone of this book to be a mixture of bouncy enthusiasm and healthy scepticism.

# CHAPTER 1

# Background to ICT in the primary school

*Bob Fox*

## Introduction

This chapter considers some of the background to the current state of ICT use in primary schools. It places the introduction of computers in an historical context, looks at different ideas about what computers are for, and discusses some of the externally imposed pressures that are brought to bear on primary practice. Most of the chapter does not relate specifically to numeracy, but the position it outlines underpins what follows in subsequent chapters.

## The historical perspective

For most of us whose memories extend back more than 20 years, the way in which we first thought about computers was probably conditioned by images from science programmes on television, or perhaps science fiction. There is an impeccably clean white room, containing a battery of large white devices that look passably like freezers, dishwashers or tumble dryers, except for the arrays of small red lights which flash sporadically, or the large spools of tape which occasionally spring to life and spin rapidly. There are a number of white-coated boffins with horn-rimmed glasses, bald heads, or both, who carry clipboards and observe, and apparently understand, what the machine is doing, and who converse with each other in some highly technical and utterly impenetrable jargon. Output from the machine is in the form of yards and yards of continuous paper containing masses of numbers and mathematical symbols. Some of the boffins scan this printout, waggle their biros at certain bits and nod sagaciously.

This is all worlds away from the daily experience of primary school teachers and children, then and now, but some of the imagery undoubtedly sits in the backs of the heads of many of the teachers who are, in Becker's (1993) terms, 'late adopters' (see also McKenzie 1999), and who have some anxieties about the place of computers in primary schools.

I built my first classroom computer in 1969. It consisted of a Shreddies box, with half of one side cut out and pushed inwards to form a chute, and a line of punched holes along the top. Knitting needles were inserted through the holes at each end, and these supported a set of index cards, also with punched holes. Each child had a card, on which they had written their name, a reference number (from 1 to 36, I think), and the yes/no answers to some simple questions – are you a boy? do you have any sisters? do you have a cat/dog/bike? and so forth. The questions were numbered, as were the holes, and where children answered a question in the affirmative a v-shaped notch was cut in the card to encompass the appropriate hole, see Figure 1.1. It was then possible to ask some questions (how many boys have dogs *and* bikes?) by inserting knitting needles through the appropriate holes, removing the supporting needles, and jiggling the computer slightly to encourage the selected cards to fall down the chute. We painted the box and stuck on some toothpaste-cap knobs to make it look more like a computer.

The mathematical concepts employed in this task were quite extensive. Apart from the actual data handling aspects – data collection, entry and verification (Sellotape was not really adequate as a means of correcting mistakes if you cut the wrong hole), prediction and hypothesis-testing, sorting and searching, graphical representation of outcomes – children had to think through the Boolean logic of complex searches in order to make the right cards fall. How do you deal with OR searches, or NOTs (as in girl = NOT boy)? Furthermore, children's reference

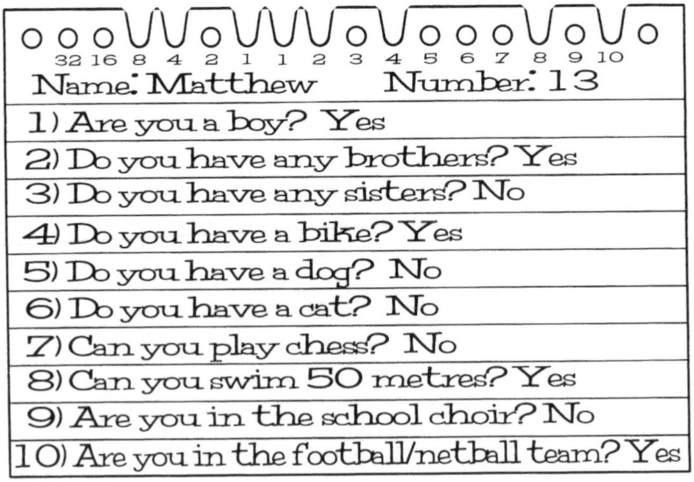

**Figure 1.1**   Card from a Shreddies computer

numbers were encoded in binary form, and holes were cut accordingly, which enabled the cards to be sorted back into alphabetical order quickly and easily, so children were getting firsthand experience of the power of binary arithmetic in a practical setting. The probability that many of the children did not completely grasp the full mathematical implications of what we were doing (I cannot even be sure that *I* did) did not diminish the validity of the exercise.

At the time, the idea of a primary school having its own *real* computer would have seemed about as far removed from reality as the idea of having its own helicopter. It would of course have been unjustifiable in terms of expense, but it was equally unjustifiable in terms of usefulness. There was simply no practical use to which it could have been put that would begin to justify the expenditure of time and effort to set up and maintain the hardware, to create curriculum space to make its use worthwhile, or to acquire the necessary skills to be able to run it. In order to become a realistic proposition, computers had to become much cheaper and much simpler to use. There also had to be some discernible reason for using them.

The history of primary school computer use is built chiefly upon developments in the first two of those conditions. The development of silicon chips and the reconceptualisation of the computer as something for individuals to use (the *personal computer*, or PC) brought about the reduction in prices, and technical developments we now take for granted (input via a keyboard, output via a monitor) made computers far more accessible. The further development of graphical user interfaces, mice, windows and icons has considerably simplified accessibility. Children currently in primary education have no more conception of a world without PCs than the rest of us have of a world without cars or aeroplanes, and operating a computer by entering instructions via a command line now looks as quaint as starting a car with a cranking handle.

Since the early 1980s we have gradually become accustomed to the notion that:

- primary schools have computers;
- then that all classrooms have computers;
- then that classes have access to several computers (for example, in a computer room or computer suite).

At the time of writing we have not yet reached the point where we assume that every child has a computer, but in one way or another we generally expect that that time will surely come. Some schools have sets of portable computers that enable children to work at their own desks, or anywhere else as the need arises. It is likely that in the longer term we will go further than that, and become accustomed to ubiquitous computing and the assumption that many devices have computers embedded in them (see for example, Weiser 1991).

All of this represents real progress, and most people would readily acknowledge the rightness and inevitability of it, given the extraordinarily rapid growth of computer technology in the world at large. What we have perhaps not managed to do is to think with sufficient power and clarity about the pedagogical implications of what computers are actually *for* in the context of the primary school. This has some consequences and repercussions, as we shall see. It can be argued that our expectations regarding primary school computer use have been developed partly according to the dictates of circumstance and partly by analogy to computer use elsewhere, whether or not this has been completely appropriate. Further, it is possible to discern, in the way some teachers and children think about the use of computers, some misconceptions or dubious preconceptions.

Before there were computers in primary schools there was already computer studies in many secondary schools. Computer studies was commonly seen as coming within the domain of mathematics departments; the majority of its proponents were male; its vocabulary was very much the vocabulary of the mainframe computer; and its content was largely geared towards understanding how computers work. It was usually a minority subject; it was not designed to be useful or even accessible to the majority of pupils. Some schools undertook computer studies before they had any computers of their own, perhaps buying time on the mainframe of an obliging local company or university. Eventually as small computers developed, secondary schools tended to acquire a few, and the notion that a secondary school might have computers in it was fairly well embedded before anyone imagined they would eventually be commonplace in primary schools. This is not to say, however, that the majority of secondary teachers made use of computers, or even that they were particularly aware of their presence or had any desire to integrate them into their daily work.

Hindsight plays tricks, and it is easy to forget that many of the things we now take for granted, like WYSIWYG ('what you see is what you get') word processing, did not exist at the point at which primary schools started to use computers. Offices were not automated or networked; calculations were not done on computerised spreadsheets; mass use of the Internet was years away. Above all, computers were severely limited by lack of memory, in ways it is difficult to comprehend now. If graphics were chunky and in plain, garish colours, this was not because that is the way programmers wanted them to look, but because that was all that the limited available memory could afford.

The introduction of computers into primary schools was precipitated by funding from the Department for Trade and Industry (DTI) and the Department of Education and Science (DES) in the early 1980s. At the time, the market for home computers was developing rapidly, and enthusiasts had a choice of a number of different systems, several of which were British in origin and design. There was no such thing as an 'industry standard' for personal computers, because the IBM-style personal computers did not exist. In selecting their DTI/DES-subsidised machine, schools were given a choice of three machines, and the BBC endorsement of the Acorn machine (the BBC 'B') made it the favourite, though by no means universal, choice.

Lucky recipients of the machines were given a short training session, which covered basics like how to plug it in, and were largely left to get on with it. Home and school computers did not have disc drives – these were still luxuries, with a three-figure price tag – and loading programs was done by means of tape cassettes. On the BBC 'B', you typed in CHAIN "", started the tape, and waited while the program loaded amid cyber-babble and the on-screen counter showed a succession of hexadecimal numbers or error messages which required you to rewind the tape and try again. Eventually, after a period of some minutes, the program started, and as often as not it was of very dubious educational value. Teachers' critical faculties were somewhat suspended, however, as it was clear that most children were highly motivated by the opportunity to use a computer, and all sorts of pedagogical limitations could be overlooked in the name of 'computer awareness'.

The way in which the new computer was used was conditioned by the fact that in most schools there was only one. This meant that it needed to be shared among classes, so rotas were established ('Class 1 on Mondays, Class 2 on Tuesdays', or 'Class 1 until Half Term', etc.) and teachers were put under pressure to make use of it while they had it, whether it fitted their plans or not. It also meant that the standard location for a computer was on a trolley on wheels, so that it could be moved from room to room, or locked away at night (at a time when people still wanted to steal such computers).

In some cases it was located within the classroom, which tended to cause a distraction as early educational programs tended to make generous use of the machine's sound facilities and colourful, flashing graphics. In other cases it was placed outside the classroom, which was also distracting for teachers, as they were frequently dragged out to assist children who were 'stuck'.

The fact that machines were shared among so many children also contributed to the common practice of expecting children to work collaboratively at the computer in twos, threes or larger groups. Perhaps most primary teachers would justify this practice by reference to the opportunities it presented for rich language interaction and the development of collaboration skills and social learning. This has often been asserted, but the evidence suggests that it may not be as simple as that (Mercer and Wegerif 1998). Perhaps the underlying reason for this organisational strategy was that it was the most effective way of ensuring that everyone had a turn in a relatively short time. This has always been, and continues to be, one of the underlying tensions in primary school computer use.

## What are computers *for* in the primary school?

Three threads which pervade early assumptions about what primary school computers are for might be considered to have been borrowed from the expanding world of home computer use:

1.  Computers are for programming.
2.  Computers are things you play games on.
3.  Computers are tools you use.

To these we might add a fourth thread, which has different origins:

4.  Computers are teaching machines.

It is slightly more conventional to identify three educational roles for the computer, characterised as 'tutor, tutee, tool' (O'Duill 1997), which would correspond to threads 4, 1 and 3. In practice our second thread will often be subsumed within the 'tutor' role (i.e. when a game purports to teach something), but it is kept separate here, because that is not always the case, and what is learned from a game may be incidental, trivial, and not transferable or relevant outside the context of the game itself.

We will explore each of these threads in turn.

## Computers are for programming

Because it took quite a long time to load a program into a computer from a tape, and because the complexity of any program was limited by the memory capacity of the machine, magazines for home computer users frequently listed short programs to type in. All home computers (and the BBC 'B') had a built-in programming language, which was usually Basic (*B*eginners' *A*ll-purpose *S*ymbolic *I*nstruction *C*ode). There was an unspoken assumption that if you bought a computer at home you would probably want to program it. In the school context, this seemed to translate into the use of the computer in lesson time, break-time or an after-school club, by the 'Enthusiasts'. It was not uncommon to find the machine being used by a couple of bright children – almost invariably boys, it seemed – armed with a small and equally bright book about how computers work.

Let us imagine, briefly, our junior programmers, sitting at the BBC 'B' trolley with their 'Let's Find Out About Computers' book. Having skimmed or skipped a number of pages showing drawings of mainframe systems, with flow diagrams labelled 'Input', 'CPU', 'Memory', etc., our programmers reach a page headed 'Writing a Program', which explains that in order to operate, computers need a sequence of instructions, known as a program, and this can be written in a number of 'languages', in this case Basic. There then follows a few lines of code, which the junior programmers are to copy (meticulously), which may well look something like this:

```
10  CLS
20  INPUT A
30  INPUT B
40  C = A*B
50  PRINT C
60  GOTO 20
```

Having typed this in, the programmers then type RUN. If they have made a mistake, they are greeted with a message like 'SYNTAX ERROR AT LINE 40'; if not, the program performs as intended. One does not need any programming experience to see what it does – the user types in two numbers, and the computer presents on the screen the product of those numbers. This activity is then repeated *ad infinitum*, or rather until they press the <Escape> key. For a while, this may be satisfying, particularly when the programmers realise they are not limited to their times tables, but can type in 4567 and 6543 to get 29881881. Perhaps they marvel at the computer's capacity to provide an answer instantly (or perhaps not – everyone now takes it for granted that computers can do that). When they try even larger numbers they find the answer is expressed in a format they can't understand (123456 $\updownarrow$ 654321 = 8.07798534E10), and after a few more goes they start to lose interest.

Or perhaps the program looks like this:

```
10  CLS
20  A = RND(10)
30  B = RND(10)
40  C = A * B
50  PRINT STR$A; "X"; STR$B;" = ";
60  INPUT D
70  IF D = C PRINT "WELL DONE!": GOTO 20
80  PRINT "TRY AGAIN": GOTO 50
    RUN
```

The reader is invited to work out what this does. We will revisit these programs at the end of the chapter.

Of course, the Enthusiasts are not actually creating these programs for themselves – they are merely typing them in. Adult passers-by will be very impressed, however, and observing the activity will no doubt reinforce their not untypical adult view that children are so much better at this sort of thing, and a major revolution in children's learning is under way. With practice, if they have a penchant for programming, the Enthusiasts may start to develop a few lines of their own code, and, after numerous syntax errors and de-buggings, they might arrive at, say, a little routine in which small graphics shapes move backwards and forwards across the screen. Those who persevere and become fluent in a computer language are on the first rung of a ladder that could lead to a possibly rewarding career somewhere in the computer industry (though perhaps not as rewarding financially as merely *selling* technology), or else to the ignominy of being labelled a nerd.

This sort of activity fizzled out in most primary schools, as it very soon became clear that this was not the sort of thing in which the majority of children were going to participate with enthusiasm, and few teachers had the knowledge, confidence or inclination to pursue this particular line beyond a fairly simple beginning. In a relatively short time there was a realisation that, though somebody has to understand this stuff, for most people, computers were something you *use*, rather than something you program. This might be thought of as the difference between designing or building a car and driving a car – or indeed being a passenger, to extend the metaphor a little further. Knowing about computers did not have to mean knowing how they worked (Turkle 1997), but, rather, knowing what they did. Perhaps the Enthusiasts pursued their programming interests at home, if they were lucky enough to own a computer – but there was relatively little acknowledgement from anyone that what they did there was substantially more intellectually demanding than anything they were required to do in school.

Because the IBM-style PC developed initially in a business context, there was never the expectation that the majority of its users would have any need to program it. Consequently PCs have no built-in high level language, and the languages in which serious computer programming is undertaken, for example C++, are as impenetrable to the layman as was the computer system in our opening scenario. The non-programmer might guess how the two short Basic programs above should work, but would be unlikely to unravel the equivalent routines in C++. As PCs now dominate the home computer market, and as our expectations of computer applications have developed to the point where they are so incredibly massive and complex that no individual could single-handedly create a commercially acceptable package, the expectation that programming might be done by people who were not professional programmers has virtually disappeared, and magazines now rarely carry listings of whole programs.

There are educational implications here, particularly for maths, since programming is largely a matter of working within a set of predefined rules in order to solve a series of logical problems. If your computer does not have a built-in programming language, you have to add one for yourself. In most primary schools the only programming language available is one that was designed for children to use – Logo. Though it has been specifically mentioned in the National Curriculum, its classroom implementation is rather patchy, and tends to depend on the enthusiasms of individual teachers or user groups, and its use is not as widespread as it deserves. Logo will be discussed in greater detail in Chapter 3.

## Computers are things you play games on

Two vignettes:
1. It is 1988. I am in a primary school corridor, fitting an InterWord word processing chip into a BBC 'B'. A small boy walks by, looks at what I am doing, and says, 'What's that game?'
2. 'Please, Miss, I've finished my work – can I play on the computer?'

However we might rationalise their purchase in terms of business use or educational value, most home computers were bought to play games on. Arcade games like Space Invaders and PacMan slightly preceded the development of the home computer, and countless 'shoot-'em-up', platform games, fighting games, flight or driving simulations, fantasy adventures, etc., have kept their users' adrenalin pumping for the last 20 years. Some games of this type may well have potential educational benefits, in terms of increased concentration, the need for complex problem-solving, and there is no doubt at all that children with computers at home have a distinct advantage over non-owners in terms of keyboard skills and general confidence with computer environments, even if all they ever do at home is zap aliens, but that in itself is not a good enough reason to base a pedagogy on the model of the computer game.

A substantial amount of classroom computer time in the last two decades has been taken up with children playing games of one sort or another on a computer. Often this has been represented as a problem-solving exercise, and sometimes the context in which the problem is couched is at least vaguely related to other subject matter being covered in class ('we are studying Romans, so everyone will play an adventure game set in Roman Britain'). All too often, particularly where the subject in hand is mathematics, the game is a drill-and-practice exercise dressed up with cartoon characters and funny special effects in an effort to make it attractive to children. A well-founded belief that children learn most effectively when they are motivated and engaged by a task is often translated into the assertion that learning is better when we make it fun, and that fun means games, so dressing up learning your times tables so that it looks like a space invaders game must necessarily be a good thing (but see for example, Postman 1985, Wiliam 1998).

There has long been the fear that children who are used to using computers as whizzy games machines will find educational programs like graph-drawing packages dull in comparison, so the well-acknowledged power of the computer as a motivator will wither unless educational software is kept as whizzy as possible. In practice, this does not actually seem to be the case for most primary children. Though they might express the view that the school computers are not as up-to-date as their home computer (which may well be true), experience so far seems to be that even an old computer with fairly dull old software is still positively motivating, and most primary children do not particularly expect or want their classrooms to be like amusement arcades.

This is not to say, of course, that dullness is a virtue in educational software, any more than it would be in, say, children's reading books. What is of primary importance, though, is fitness for purpose, and a game which does not teach what it purports to teach at least as efficiently as could have been achieved by other methods is probably not worth using. Some games simply waste time. An early example of this was a game which was sited, apparently, in a robot-making factory.

The robot raw materials on a conveyor belt bore a number. As the bits passed into the robot-manufacturing machine, the users had to multiply the number by 2 and type in the answer. If the correct number had been entered, a splendid robot appeared at the far end; if not, a bent robot emerged. This was fun for about two minutes, if rather repetitive. However, the whole process of making a set of robots took about ten minutes, during which time the users had practised the two times table once. One reads much about the capacity of computers to motivate children who are not normally enthusiastic about schoolish things like maths, but, as we shall see, if mathematics lessons are conducted briskly and with the direct engagement of all participants, there are really very few children who are so completely unmotivated that they require an expensive machine, and a task wrapped up to look like something else, to make them participate at all.

Another early assumption about educational games was that pupils should receive some sort of reward for getting the answers right or for completing the activity (or puzzle, or adventure). It would be easy to dismiss this as merely crude behaviourism, but the fact remains that most people like to engage in activities that challenge their capabilities, to compete against themselves or against others, and to receive some form of affirmation when they achieve their goal or better their performance. This reasoning could of course be applied to the crossword puzzle or the jigsaw, neither of which is required to make noises or flash lights when completed.

In looking at educational games software, what we need to consider is whether that achievement has any meaning or value outside its immediate context, and specifically whether the attainment of the goal actually represents any development in understanding or the learning of transferable skills. If not, why give valuable curriculum space to it?

Vignette number 3 – the games-playing teacher's anxiety (anecdotally reported in one form or another by several computer enthusiasts):

> 'It's half past one in the morning, I have to be up at seven o'clock in order to teach at nine, and I'm still desperately trying to make these silly falling shapes fit together so that I can get a score on the highscore board – what am I *doing?*'

## Computers are tools you use

Most people who have access to a computer in their professional lives use it as a tool. The software with which they are familiar exists to enable them to undertake a task quicker, easier or better than they could have done it by other means. Most adult computer users are familiar with the main functions of a word processor; many people use spreadsheets to organise numerical data; the use of fax, e-mail and the Internet is now standard practice in most office environments. Generally, users receive sufficient training in the use of a specific software package to enable them to function effectively in their work. It does not follow that they know anything else about ICT beyond the confines in which they operate, and they would generally look elsewhere for support if for any reason their system did not operate as they expected it to.

Many of the most worthwhile ways of using a computer in the primary school also entail thinking of it as a tool. It is easy (though beyond the present remit) to justify the use of a word processor as a tool to support and enhance children's writing, and, as we shall see, databases, spreadsheets and graphing programs are all relevant to the teaching of maths. The content-free nature of such software makes it flexible and capable of being used in a variety of ways and for a variety of purposes. What needs to be kept in balance is the tension between learning *about* an application and learning *with* it. In many classrooms where ICT is seen as important, a lot of energy has been expended on teaching children how to use an application, and on getting to grips with techniques that are specific and local to that application, and the aims of such lessons are expressed in terms of acquiring those techniques. Relatively little time has been spent on putting those techniques to good use to enhance learning in another subject. It is surely the case that neither approach should exist in a vacuum – that learning techniques for their own sake is pointless, but equally that attempting to make use of a software tool without a sufficient grasp of the techniques needed to drive it is almost invariably frustrating and counter-productive. We will return to this point later.

## Computers are teaching machines

The idea of using a computer as a teaching machine is very seductive, but for different reasons to different groups of people. The development of an earlier generation of teaching machines in America in the 1960s was based on the work of behaviourist psychologist B. F. Skinner. The idea was that learning could be tailored to meet the needs of individuals, as the machine could determine what question to ask next in response to a pupil's answers. This might be fine if you believe that learning is about the transmission of information, and if you believe that it proceeds in a more-or-less linear and pre-definable manner, and if the machine is sufficiently subtle and has a large enough set of questions to cater appropriately for all eventualities. The machines of the 1960s were not successful in America, and made no significant impression in Britain; but much the same sort of thinking, albeit at a much more sophisticated level, underpins the development of computer-based Integrated Learning Systems in recent years. These are discussed in greater depth in Chapter 3.

The fear (or hope, depending on your perspective) that computers could eventually replace teachers is based on a naive understanding of what is involved in the process of teaching and learning, and a limited concept of the nature of knowledge. Much recent thinking (and the National Numeracy Strategy in particular) has stressed the central importance of the teacher (Tabberer 1997). This is not to say that computers cannot be effective in the role of tutor, however. What seems to matter most is the extent to which the teacher is involved in what happens when children use computers. This is a central theme of this book.

In the worst practice, teachers seem happy to hand over responsibility for teaching to the machine, and do not feel obliged to monitor or assess precisely what happens. There is no need for them to become familiar with the operation or content of the software. This is the 'go over there and get on with that' approach to ICT, the computer-as-childminder. For the technology-shy teacher who needs to be seen to be using ICT but who does not have time to become familiar with what the software can do, this approach has a certain appeal, and it is very much the easy option – but it is often a waste of everybody's time.

## Three types of imposition

The central point of this chapter is that the way in which we conceptualise ICT in primary education is governed initially by historical preconceptions about what sort of thing a computer is and what it might be for, but it is also substantially coloured by external factors which impose themselves for reasons which are not necessarily rooted in pedagogy. As Benzie (1995) puts it, 'With IT, there is a huge danger that control … will be taken by those whose first loyalty is not to teaching and learning.'

Three types of imposition are discussed here. The first two deal with pressures that are external to teaching, and the third addresses the expectations and constraints under which classroom practitioners are obliged to operate. Some of those expectations look like golden opportunities, but that does not mean that they are without problems or inherent stresses. Some of what follows is intentionally provocative, and challenges what appears to be current received wisdom. It might usefully form the basis for discussion in a lecture, staff meeting or INSET session.

## 1. The Technological Imperative

The Technological Imperative is the unvoiced assumption, seemingly held by many people, that if it is technically possible to do something, it is therefore desirable or even essential to do it. Thus each new innovation in computer technology must by definition be a 'good thing', and should be incorporated in school policy at the earliest opportunity (Fox 1997).

It is the Technological Imperative that expects that primary school ICT use should include:

- networking, though in probably the majority of primary schools there is no-one with the time or expertise to manage a network effectively, and potential advantages to be gained by networking machines can easily be outweighed by the inconvenience of rendering all the school's computers simultaneously unusable whenever the network goes down;
- the Internet, though particularly in Early Years contexts no-one has yet demonstrated sufficient worthwhile educational benefits to justify the considerable expense – as McKenzie (1999) puts it, schools 'have hooked up to the Internet as if it were some magnificent "digital library" instead of an "information yard-sale"';
- video-conferencing – what for?

Of course, one can make out plausible cases for the potential inclusion of all the above, and technology enthusiasts generally look for opportunities to absorb new ideas into their current practice and experiment with possibilities. Networks can make it easier to share substantial software packages around a school; the National Grid for Learning (NGfL) will eventually make the Internet a far more focused and worthwhile source of information and resources. But, for the technology-shy teacher, they reinforce the sense that something is being imposed from outside. They represent a model of computer use that might be appropriate in a different context (say, an office environment), but which should not simply be accepted uncritically as the 'right thing to do'. According to McKenzie (1999), 'networking has virtually removed the notion of teachers as customers with choices. They awaken one day with computers in their rooms without having requested them.'

## 2. Pressures of the market – hardware and software

Who owns ICT? The correct answer, of course, is nobody. There can be no single body which is the ultimate arbiter of correctness, appropriateness and good practice. Since the first computers arrived in primary schools, the computer industry in the world at large has grown stupendously, and millions of people worldwide earn their living either directly or indirectly from that industry. Set against that, the scale of ICT in primary education is minuscule, and it is hardly surprising that pressures from the market influence what happens in primary schools. For several years Acorn computers were the dominant machines in primary schools, but they remained virtually unheard of in all other spheres (for reasons that were perhaps more to do with marketing than anything else). A common jibe from computer buffs from outside the world of education was that school hardware and software was not 'industry standard', with the implication that this therefore made it inferior in some way – never mind that the machines were still in daily use after 10 or 15 years, and much of the best-known software was appropriately matched to the learning needs of young children. There is no particular reason to view 'industry standard' (whatever that means) as a recommendation for school use, any more than labelling something 'educational standard' would recommend it to industry. The jibe seemed to be based on the assumption that the main reason for using ICT in the primary school is to prepare children for the world of work. Categorically, it is not. Owen (1999) points out that the fork lift truck is 'industry standard' transport!

The steady rise of the PC in schools and the eventual demise of Acorn as a company has meant that the balance has shifted, and virtually all new computers bought for schools in England are now PCs (Apple computers, which hold a fairly dominant position in American schools, have been more common in Scotland than in England, though there are pockets of Apple users in some English areas). One of the potential advantages of convergence on one platform will be an increase in compatibility between machines children use in school and at home.

## (a) Hardware

Computer manufacturers exist not to design and sell the perfect computer which would meet all users' needs forever, but to go on selling computers, each one marginally better (i.e. faster and more powerful) than the last. The time scale after which PCs are considered to be obsolete is variously quoted as two years, eighteen months, nine months, etc. Arguably, machines are in some respects obsolete even before they are available for sale. To date, the world of business and industry has more or less managed to pay for the rapid pace of change through improvements in productivity and efficiency generated by the technology. Schools do not work like that, and it is probably unrealistic to expect that they will 'keep pace' at all. Indeed, there are still 1982-vintage BBC 'B's in daily use in primary classrooms!

We need to examine why we might wish primary schools to keep pace with technological innovation. Five reasons might be:

1. Because children need to understand the use of technology in the wider community. This is a commonly expressed view, but it is not a particularly compelling reason to insist on always having the latest or best equipment. Schools are not obliged to have their own nuclear submarines in order for pupils to know what they are and what they do. The Technological Imperative would have all primary classrooms linked by video-conferencing, though until such time as there are clearly demonstrable educational benefits to be had, this seems a rather dubious and potentially expensive deviation from the general business of the primary classroom. We would be doing it because it can be done, rather than because it is worth doing. There is, of course, a fair chance that a future reader of this chapter may find this particular assertion quaint and naive. In secondary schools,

particularly at the upper end, there is perhaps a pressing need for pupils to know about applications they might encounter in the world of work. There is nothing you could teach a class of eight-year-olds now about particular computers or software that will still be relevant by the time they are in full-time employment.

2.  Because many children will have up-to-date equipment at their disposal at home, and may therefore be dissatisfied with, or even demotivated by, outdated school equipment. There may well be some children for whom this is at least partially true – and many children have a range of high-tech toys at their disposal with which we would not particularly expect classroom resources to compete – but in general children seem to find computers motivating, however old they may be.

3.  Because support for older equipment (in the sense of maintenance or the availability of parts or consumables) cannot be guaranteed. This is, regrettably, a valid reason for not permitting school equipment to fall too far behind the market-place. It is also an excellent reason for treating with caution schemes by which schools are given second-hand, almost-obsolete hardware from industrial sources.

4.  Because new resources and teaching materials make assumptions about the media through which they will be used (a prime example of this is the production of software in CD–ROM format only, on the assumption that everyone has the necessary drives). This reason also has some validity. The storage capacity of CD–ROM is such that it makes possible the use of much bigger files than can be accommodated on a floppy disc. In practice, this has often meant higher quality graphics, video clips or animations. For all the claims that are made about 'interactivity', however, high-quality graphics on a CD–ROM do not necessarily improve the quality of the learning experience, any more than the introduction of colour improved the educational value of television. At times we seem to be in danger of allowing curriculum content to be dictated by encyclopaedia salesmen.

5.  Because technological innovation opens up new horizons for learning. This ought to be the best reason – however, it is often the case that the technology drives the pedagogy, rather than the other way round. In an ideal world, the two would work in harmony. There have been many over-optimistic claims for the efficacy of new technologies. Cuban (1986) showed that film, radio and television were all predicted to precipitate a rapid and radical change in the way education was conducted, and all failed to do so for reasons which prompt a feeling of *déjà vu* – cost, inadequacy of equipment, lack of training, and so forth, but particularly because the rationale for the technological change came from non-teachers.

The government strategy for overcoming the problem of hardware redundancy is for schools to take on managed systems, which would involve passing responsibility for maintenance, repairs and replacement of hardware to an outside agency. It remains to be seen whether (a) this is affordable, particularly by small primary schools, and (b) whether the resulting removal of anxiety and stress compensates for the accompanying loss of autonomy.

### (b) Software

The market for educational software in the United Kingdom is not huge. Primary schools do not expect to pay high prices for software, and indeed do not have the funds to do so. When the first wave of computers arrived in schools, a number of textbook publishers started to add software titles to their catalogues, but when it became apparent that there were no fortunes to be made in the school market, many withdrew. Among the firms that persevered were some that were set up and staffed by ex-teachers. Additionally, software was produced by education insiders in projects like the Microelectronics Education Project (MEP). This meant that for a number of years a substantial amount of software for primary schools was designed by people who had some insight into the way schools operate, and, more crucially, who were familiar with the assumptions UK primary teachers make about the way children learn. It was possible for several years to treat educational software design and production as a cottage industry, and many of the best-known and best-loved pieces of primary software were written by programmers working singly or in pairs. Budget restrictions meant that there was no possibility of devoting to a single program the thousands of hours of research and development or the huge programming teams that have become the norm when creating a package for business use or a modern computer game for the home market.

While the majority of primary school computers were Acorn machines, virtually all the software in common use was British in origin; indeed, many of the best and most popular school programs on the PC were re-versioned Acorn programs. This was not true of 'educational' software intended for the home computer market, however, much of which was American in origin. There is nothing inherently wrong with Americanness *per se* (indeed, Logo is mostly an American concept), and this paragraph does not intend to suggest that there is not an abundance of appropriately-designed educational software written for the PC, but a large proportion of what purports to be educational software for the home market, whatever its country of origin, seems almost entirely lacking in that informed understanding of children's learning that has characterised British educational software from the mid-1980s onwards. Objections to such software might be:

- that it often over-simplifies and trivialises the process of learning, often reducing it to the regurgitation of 'facts' for their own sake;
- that it frequently mistakes testing for teaching;
- that, in order to appeal to a mass market, it elevates 'fun' above serious learning intentions – hence the description of much of it as 'edutainment';

- that few of the skills it would claim to develop can be shown to have translated into real, long-term improvements in children's academic performance.

Another pressure that should be resisted is the temptation to fit the child to the software rather than the software to the child. This may come about because of the dominant market position of some serious software applications, which, though they may be excellent in the context for which they were designed, are not actually well-geared to the learning needs of primary children. Though children can undoubtedly be taught to use them, they do not relate well to the preoccupations of the classroom, and lack a 'pedagogic layer', and one is left with the feeling that children are learning *about* the software rather than learning *with* it (see above). This is not to say, however, that children should not have access to complex software where its use is appropriate to, or required by, the intended learning outcome – merely that the learning outcome should not be principally determined by what the software can do. The same is equally true of over-simple software, of course.

## (3) Expectations

### (a) Value for money in learning gains
Computers are relatively expensive items, and the money spent on them by governments, local authorities, parents and others could have bought a host of other resources. An enormous amount of faith has been invested in the expectation that the expense will be justified in terms of improved standards in one form or another, but as yet the evidence for this is less than compelling. The assumption is nicely crystallised by Russell (1995): 'If learners (at any level, any age, any gender, any grade, any IQ, etc.) are taught [some computer application] (for any length of time, using any method, by any teacher, etc.), they will improve more in [some cognitive or performance variable] than an experimental group who are taught traditionally [whatever that is].'

In an educational climate which has increasingly viewed school and teacher accountability in terms of measurable gains in pupil performance, this creates a dilemma, particularly for the technology-shy teacher: 'I must be seen to improve children's performance, and I must be seen to use ICT to do it, but the evidence that it works just isn't there.'

### (b) The National Curriculum
For the first few years of their existence in school, there was no clear definition of the role of computers in the curriculum; for one thing, it was not realistic to insist that they should be used in every class, since there were not sufficient machines to

ensure that that would happen; also, it is easy to forget that before the coming of the National Curriculum nothing was compulsory anyway.

The first version of the National Curriculum included Information Technology almost as an afterthought, as the fifth Attainment Target within Technology (DES 1990). It was only after the Dearing review (Dearing 1994) that it emerged as a subject in its own right. There were, however, sporadic references to the use of computers in the programmes of study for a number of subjects, though very little was specified in detail, again because it would have been unenforceable. The post-Dearing version of the National Curriculum included a reference to the use of ICT in the preamble to every subject (except PE), stating that it should be used 'where appropriate', but giving no indication of how such appropriateness might be determined. Since 1998 ICT has been identified as a core subject. Because it is a National Curriculum subject, all pupils have a statutory right to be taught it.

In the mid-1980s the idea that ICT could be both a subject in its own right and also a means of delivering other subjects was not problematic, as over the previous 20 years teachers had become accustomed to the idea of interaction among different curricular elements. Successive governments' insistence on framing the curriculum more strictly in terms of subjects has left ICT in a slightly odd position. The Stevenson Report (Stevenson 1996), commissioned by the Labour Party before they came to power in 1997, coined the term Information and Communications Technology, adding Communications to the previous name (Information Technology) in acknowledgement that electronic communications, and the Internet in particular, would make a significant impression on learning, as on life in general; for a while the two terms were used interchangeably, as synonyms. The matter was subsequently 'clarified' by designating IT as the National Curriculum subject, and ICT as the medium that could be used to enhance teaching and learning in all subjects. After the 2000 revision of the National Curriculum the term ICT will take on both meanings.

### (c) The National Grid for Learning, and great expectations

Since the General Election of 1997 the Government has promoted a succession of initiatives, each intended to create a rapid and significant change in the educational use of ICT. The aim of the National Grid for Learning is to ensure that every school in the country has access to the Internet (see Chapter 4). The funding attached to it has provided a considerable quantity of hardware for schools, and ensured that network cabling is installed. The arrival of new money for computers has coincided with a growing anxiety about the proportion of IT lessons judged by OFSTED to be unsatisfactory, and in many schools the solution to the problem has been to place all the new machines in one area, and establish a computer room or suite.

As long as a school has physical space available, a computer room is an attractive proposition, for a number of reasons. The first reason, though not necessarily the most important consideration, is that it is a great deal cheaper and easier to provide network cabling in one centralised room than it is to cable an entire building. The second reason is that a computer room allows the whole class (or perhaps half the class, depending on circumstance) to use computers simultaneously, thus eliminating many of the problems associated with having to wait days or weeks for one's turn on the solitary classroom machine. It becomes much easier and more efficient to teach IT as a National Curriculum subject if there is a computer room available. If classes are timetabled to use the room at a particular time of the week, it helps to focus teachers' attention on the structuring of their children's ICT experiences. In some schools, ICT coordinators are able to make use of the computer room to provide training for their less confident colleagues. On the other hand, if the setting up of a computer room leads to the removal of computers from individual classes, much may have been lost, in terms of the capacity for spontaneity generally, and specifically in relation to the use of ICT to support teaching and learning in literacy and numeracy. These points for Numeracy will be elaborated further in Chapters 3 and 5.

Running more or less in parallel with the establishment of the National Grid for Learning is the provision of training in ICT for all teachers, funded via the National Lottery (the funding source is conventionally referred to as the New Opportunities Fund, or NOF). Some £230 million is being made available, between 1999 and 2002, to provide training for all serving teachers in the use of ICT in core subjects. This works out at approximately £450 per head, which does not seem an adequate sum, given the scale of the task to be accomplished.

At the same time, undergraduate and postgraduate students on teaching courses are required to meet in full all the specifications laid out in Annex B of DfEE Circular 4/98 (DfEE 1998c) with regard to personal ICT skills and teaching and learning in core subjects and specialist subjects with ICT. Any students who do not satisfactorily demonstrate that they meet all the requirements will not be awarded Qualified Teacher Status. The intended outcomes of the NOF training are expressed in the same terms.

One fairly large problem that is beginning to emerge is the mismatch between an effect of the NGfL (putting all the machines in one place) and the requirements of both Circular 4/98 and the NOF training that teachers should make use of ICT to enhance teaching and learning in core subjects. As 'core subjects' includes the literacy hour and the daily mathematics lesson, and as these are generally taking place simultaneously throughout a school, it is difficult to see how ICT can be incorporated in them if there are no computers left in the classroom. In an ideal world, of course, there will be computers in both the computer room and the classroom. This issue is discussed in greater depth in Chapter 5.

One insight about computer use which has become accepted wisdom in recent years is that teachers are more likely to make use of ICT in their classes if they are themselves computer owners and users. Government-funded schemes have run to provide laptop computers, initially for head teachers and senior staff, and the eventual aim will be to ensure that all teachers have computers of their own.

Though one should no doubt feel pleased at the extent to which ICT is being supported and promoted by the above initiatives, they do nevertheless impose external pressure on teachers, many of whom feel far from confident about the use of ICT in the classroom. It is difficult to see how training at the level proposed could possibly transform the teaching profession as a whole into ICT enthusiasts. In the past, support for ICT has rarely extended beyond the provision of hardware and software, and such training as has been possible has tended to focus on the acquisition of technical skills rather than on considerations of classroom practice (Harris 1999).

## Teachers' confidence, and resistance to change

Cuban (1986) showed that, historically, new technologies imposed on education from outside have made far less difference than their proponents predicted. This is partly to do with ownership of change, and with teachers' perceptions of what their problems are and how best they might be overcome. Many teachers would subscribe to the view that, in McKenzie's (1999) phrase, if your class is not broken, why fix it?

Successive reports from HMI and OFSTED have indicated that overall the level of ICT teaching in primary schools is weak by comparison with other subjects, and that there are very substantial differences between schools, and between classes in the same school. Though there are pockets of good practice, there are far too many examples of ICT being used badly, insufficiently or not at all. 'On the one hand, the microcomputer has been an agent of curriculum development … On the other hand, the microcomputer has been an intrusion, entering the classroom in a manner that bears resemblance to the zealous missionary activity in "heathen" lands in the nineteenth century. Too often the hardware promoted and the software produced appear to pay too little attention to the value and validity of current classroom practice' (Baker 1985).

For many primary teachers the developed skill of teaching is closely bound up with knowing how to handle human interactions at a personal or group level, and this does not sit very comfortably alongside the image of the computer as something related to boffins, science, complicated mathematics, technical expertise, and very left-brained logical activity.

There have been various attempts to classify teachers' approaches to ICT use. Rhodes, for example, categorises them as enthusiasts, dabblers, conformists, marginalists and the disenchanted (see Cox 1997). However the classification is done, the proportion who are identified as enthusiasts, or, in Becker's (1993) terms, 'early adopters', is always a minority. The rest approach it with varying degrees of reluctance. Though most primary teachers do in fact make regular use of ICT, with the majority doing so twice a week or more (Harris 1999), most feel they lack the competence or confidence to do so effectively. Many primary teachers will readily admit that they 'don't really understand ICT', and will blame or excuse themselves by saying 'I'm not very computer-literate, I'm afraid'. They do not seem to relate what they do to what computers do; computers present for them a challenge they do not feel able to match, even if their classroom computers are in use for much of the time. Brosnan (1998) points out technophobes are not necessarily non-computer-users. Though they feel they should make more use of computer technology, their anxieties tend to focus (sometimes understandably) on the unreliability of hardware and software ('It's all right if it's working, but what happens when it goes wrong?'). They cite lack of equipment, outdated equipment, lack of appropriate software, no time to learn how to use software, no technical support. Computer use is mostly thought of in terms of acquiring IT skills, and there is generally little appreciation of the potential of ICT to enhance teaching and learning in other subjects. ICT is seen as a bolt-on extra, in Loveless's (1995a) phrase, 'another plate to spin'.

Perhaps more alarmingly, even where teachers declare themselves comfortable with the use of ICT it does not follow that what is actually being done is worthwhile. An NCET project on developing higher-order information handling skills found that even among schools which had been nominated for their interest, 'few ... seemed able to use IT to challenge pupils' thinking or to promote and enhance learning' (NCET 1997). A large proportion of word-processing time still seems to be no more than merely copying up previously written text; there is plenty of evidence for computer use unrelated to the matter-in-hand of the lesson (children simply take it in turns to have a go at the computer game). A leading primary software producer informed the present author that their market research indicated that teachers were not interested in data handling software, so they did not produce any.

There are clearly problems here. We will explore the implications of them later in the book. To round off this chapter, however, we will return to the programming activity of our two Enthusiasts.

## Thinking about computer programs and programming

In discussing what computers might be for, we mentioned, in passing, three roles they can adopt: tutor, tutee and tool. As an exercise, you are invited to explore the two short programs listed on pages 6 and 7. This could form part of a lecture, staff meeting or in-service course. As you complete this exercise, keep in mind your own views about what computers are for in the primary school. Do not read the points below until you have completed the task.

If you have an Acorn machine to hand (or any other computer with Basic built in), try typing in each program (you may think you do not have a suitable machine, but there are still some serviceable BBC 'B's lurking in the back of classroom cupboards). If you do not have access to a machine with Basic, examine the listings carefully, and decide how you would go about making the proposed modifications.

If you are using an Archimedes (A3000, etc.) or RISC PC you will need to hit function key f12 first, set the Caps Lock on, and type Basic <Return>. When you have finished with one program and wish to type in the other, you will need to type NEW <Return>. Run the programs for a while, and reflect on what you think using computers in maths teaching is actually about.

Even if you have never programmed a computer before, try these modifications:

- re-write the first program so that it adds instead of multiplying;
- re-write the second program so that it adds (with numbers up to 100) instead of multiplying;
- re-write the second program so that it adds three numbers.

Hint: to avoid having to re-write the whole program many times, you can use LIST <Return> to list the program lines, re-type any line you wish to modify, hit <Return>, then type LIST <Return> again to see your revised program. Remember to type RUN <Return> to test your program. When you have finished, Archimedes users will need to hit <Escape> and type *QUIT <Return> <Return> to get back to the desktop.

Do not read on until you have completed the task.

Points to consider:

1. Unless you were already quite a fluent programmer, you will have learned something about programming. Programming is a problem-solving activity within a rule-based framework. You may have learned that instructions have to be expressed exactly and unambiguously, according to the rules; and unless you have been very lucky or very clear-sighted, you will have made the modifications by means of trial and error.

2. It is hoped that you have been successful, and feel good about the experience; in particular, it is hoped that you did not give up in panic the first time you discovered you were guilty of a SYNTAX ERROR. You may well have learned that programming is something you personally do not need to do.

3. If you were successful in conducting the modifications to the second program, you may even have considered the possibility of making some other modifications of your own – in which case you will be aware that programming is potentially a flexible and highly creative activity. Bear this in mind when you consider Logo in Chapter 3.

4.  As you typed in the programs, or more particularly as you modified them, the computer was adopting the role of tutee. For many creative activities this is the role the computer adopts.

5.  The first program could be thought of as a simple tool – a very limited calculator, in fact. Within the set of rules within which it is operating (which you determined by writing the program), the computer is the agent of your wishes. It enables you to extend your own capabilities, and could potentially be useful to you in any context in which you wished to employ it.

6.  Within similarly limited terms, the second program could be thought of as a game. It contains no time limitations, no points to be scored, no defined end-point, and no automatic progression in difficulty, but it issues you with a constant (if uninteresting) set of challenges.

7.  It is not, of course, teaching you anything, except insofar as you might improve your recall skills if you can manage to play it for long enough. It is not a problem-solving exercise, and requires no creative imagination on your part. It might be thought of as a drill-and-practice program, but it is not really acting as a tutor.

8.  The computer controls the activity, by choosing the question and verifying the answer. As you used the program, how did you feel about the randomness of the question choice? If the choice is completely random (as it is here, within the parameters you have set), there is nothing to stop it from asking you a succession of hard questions followed by a succession of easy questions, or the same question repeatedly.

9.  A more subtle program might grade questions by level of difficulty (which invariably seems to correlate with the size of the numbers used, so, for example, multiplying by 10 might be categorised as harder than multiplying by 4). A very subtle program, for example some Integrated Learning Systems (see Chapter 3), would make decisions about what questions to ask in the light of the user's responses. At some level, however, the question will still be random within the parameters set.

10. However the question is determined, the verification of the answer can only be made in terms of *what* you answer; it can take little account of *how* you do so. Most particularly, if you make an incorrect response, the extent to which a computer can analyse *why* it is incorrect is severely limited.

11. What this is leading to is an absolutely crucial point – that effective learning very often depends on mediation by a teacher. It is simply not good enough to say to children, 'go over there and get on with that, and don't bother me.'

12. As you consider the various types of software discussed in later chapters, consider whether at root they add anything of substance to these two little programs, or whether that addition is mere froth and bubble.

CHAPTER 2

# Mathematics teaching and learning: past, present and future

*Ann Montague-Smith*

This chapter considers the implications of international comparisons in mathematics achievement, teachers' beliefs and values, and the implications of the introduction of the National Numeracy Strategy. Recent practice in the use of ICT, including software and calculators, is reviewed, and the expectations of the National Numeracy Framework for ICT considered.

## International and national comparisons of mathematical performance

Surveys of attainment in mathematics were not carried out systematically until the late 1970s. It is surmised (Foxman 1998) that there was probably an improvement in arithmetic performance in the 10 to 15 years following the end of the Second World War, and that performance began to fall after that and continued to do so into the 1990s. International surveys of mathematics at age 13 were carried out, starting in 1964 to the present, and showed that the pattern of performance for England, Wales and Scotland was similar. Britain's performance was below that of the Pacific Rim countries and behind that of the highest performing European countries such as Switzerland (Foxman 1998).

In 1992 Foxman *et al.* (1992), showed that England's peformance was well below that of Hungary, Korea and Taiwan. The performance of these three countries was considered in the data analysed by Reynolds (1996) where he showed that there were significant differences in attitude, classroom management and pedagogy for mathematics teaching which may account for their higher performance.

The Assessment of Performance Unit (APU), set up within the former Department of Education and Science (DES), commissioned surveys of performance in England, Wales and Northern Ireland and found that between 1982 and 1987 there were improvements in performance in Geometry, Handling Data and Measures, and a decline in Number and Algebra. There was considerable concern about the performance of children in England and Wales (though not in Scotland, which was considered to provide a good standard of education by the government), as evidenced through employers' concerns about the standards of arithmetic shown by apprentices and other workers.

The response to this in the mid 1980s was the setting up of the National Curriculum, with its introduction for mathematics for Year 1 children in September 1989 (Sawyer 1993), with revised orders issued in 1991 and 1995 (DES 1989b, DES 1991, DfE 1995). Children are formally assessed at the end of each key stage, and results for Key Stages 2 and 3, and GCSE, are published each year. However, these tests have changed in format over time, and with a separate curriculum and assessment body for each of England, Wales, Scotland and Northern Ireland, it is not possible to look at British results; instead each country must be considered individually. In England the Schools Curriculum and Assessment Authority (SCAA) has tried to maintain comparable assessment standards each year (Foxman 1998). Similarly, GCSE and A level results are compared year on year, and tables of performance are produced each year, with results for A levels showing a small increase in pass rate each year. However, results of a study by Davies and Brember (1999) have shown that there has been stability in the results for Year 2 children over a period of eight years, which suggests that instead of raising standards, the purpose in implementing the National Curriculum, these have remained the same. It is conjectured by Davies and Brember that the National Curriculum has restricted the available time for teaching basic skills, including those of mathematics.

The Third International Mathematics and Science Study (TIMSS), in 1995, showed that England had a differential in performance between Science and Mathematics at age 18, with England performing better in Science than in Mathematics. The results were similar for 9- and 13-year-olds. Figure 2.1 shows England ranked seventeenth out of 26 for Mathematics, but eighth out of 26 for Science. The top section in the table achieved mean scores significantly higher than England. The shaded section achieved mean scores very similar to England. The bottom section achieved mean scores significantly lower than England.

From the international surveys for 1991–5, teachers reported that they considered that they gave high emphasis to number operations, but this was in conflict with the results from the surveys which showed England performing at a below average level for Number and above average in Handling Data and Geometry. These results have led to the rethinking of how Number should be

| SCIENCE | MATHEMATICS |
|---|---|
| Korea | Singapore |
| Japan | Korea |
| USA | Japan |
| Austria | Hong Kong |
| Australia | The Netherlands |
| The Netherlands | Czech Republic |
| Czech Republic | Austria |
| **ENGLAND** | Slovenia |
| Canada | Ireland |
| Singapore | Hungary |
| Slovenia | Australia |
| Ireland | USA |
| Scotland | Canada |
| Hong Kong | Israel |
| Hungary | Latvia (LSS) |
| New Zealand | Scotland |
| Norway | **ENGLAND** |
| Latvia (LSS) | Cyprus |
| Israel | Norway |
| Iceland | New Zealand |
| Greece | Greece |
| Portugal | Thailand |
| Cyprus | Portugal |
| Thailand | Iceland |
| Iran, Islamic Republic | Iran, Islamic Republic |
| Kuwait | Kuwait |

**Figure 2.1**   England's ranking in international mathematics tests (taken from Keys 1998)

taught and learnt in primary schools (Foxman 1998). However, there is evidence (*TES*, 20 August 1999), of a 10 per cent age point improvement in the proportion of pupils reaching expected standards in mathematics in SAT scores, as reported by their Local Educational Authorities (LEAs).

## Defining numeracy

What is numeracy? The general public use terms such as arithmetic, sums, number, to describe the knowledge, understanding and use of numbers. The term 'numeracy' is not used in the 1989, 1991 or 1995 National Curricula, instead the mathematics curriculum is considered under the headings of Number, Algebra, Shape and Space, Measures and Handling Data (DES 1989b, DES 1991, DfE 1995). A working definition used by the Askew *et al.* (1997) report for the Teacher Training Agency is: 'Numeracy is the ability to process, communicate and interpret numerical information in a variety of contexts.'

This clearly suggests that it is the knowledge, understanding and use of numbers in context which defines this concept. The definition used by the DfEE in the reports from the Numeracy Task Force (1998a, 1998d) is that used by the National Numeracy Strategy (1999) and is seen as defining the essence of the concepts and skills which make someone numerate and the definition is seen as parallel to that of literacy and being literate: 'Numeracy is a proficiency which involves confidence and competence with numbers and measures. It requires an understanding of the number system, a repertoire of computational skills and an inclination and ability to solve number problems in a variety of contexts. Numeracy also demands practical understanding of the ways in which information is gathered by counting and measuring, and is presented in graphs, diagrams, charts and tables.' This definition of numeracy does not cover all aspects of mathematics; for example it makes no mention of shape and space. However, The National Numeracy Strategy (DfEE 1999) does include shape and space in its Framework.

## The importance of numeracy

In England it has, for many years, been culturally acceptable to admit to finding mathematics (numbers, arithmetic, algebra) difficult, or even incomprehensible, and thus to be innumerate, whereas it is not socially acceptable to be illiterate. Cockcroft (1982) found that by the age of 11 there was a seven year gap in performance between the most and least able as evidenced by a high school head of mathematics: 'You must remember that we are dealing with an ability spread of Level 1 to Level 7 for our 11-year-olds' (Sawyer 1993).

Since the industrial revolution, with the move of the population towards town and city dwelling and away from the country, the management of personal finances has become more and more important. As was said of Mr Micawber in *David Copperfield* by Charles Dickens in 1850, 'Annual income twenty pounds, annual expenditure nineteen nineteen six, result happiness, Annual income twenty pounds, annual expenditure twenty pounds ought and six, result misery.' Whilst much manual labour did not require numerate employees, that position has changed over recent years, and the Institute of Manpower Studies (Atkinson *et al.* 1993) found in a survey of employers that seven out of eight jobs have some numeracy requirements. Whilst these skills could be learnt on the job, this would lead to a very narrow range of numeracy skills, those specific to the particular job. In today's job market, where people may need to change the nature of their work more than once during their working life, this approach would not be effective. Bynner and Parsons (1997) showed that 25 per cent of the adults surveyed by the Basis Skills Agency had such poorly developed numeracy skills that this would make the completion of everyday tasks difficult and that only 9 per cent of these people recognised their difficulties compared with 19 per cent of people with poor literacy skills. Today, with the easy access to information through television, radio, newspapers, books, magazines and the Internet, people need to be able to understand the data offered and to interpret its meaning. They need to be able to compare sets of figures and decide whether they are accurate, or which one represents the best value for them. The government, through its Numeracy Task Force report (DfEE 1998), has shown its determination to raise standards of numeracy so that Britain improves its standing in international comparative studies and has a well trained workforce which can meet the international demands of the twenty-first century. The expectation is that the population will have a wide range of numeracy skills, will be able to calculate mentally, as well as use paper and pencil, and will understand how the number system works and use this knowledge to solve problems.

The importance of being numerate in order to be a successful adult member of society is part of the culture of those countries that do so much better than Britain in the international comparisons. In Taiwan parents have high aspirations for their children and so expect them to be fully numerate. In Switzerland there is a concentration on basic number work. In Taiwan, Switzerland and Hungary there are high expectations of what all children can achieve (Reynolds 1996). However, the workload of teachers in other countries may be different from that of British teachers. For example, in Beijing, mathematics teaching is marked by the highly-structured lessons, and the very thorough preparation undertaken by teachers who have a much lighter teaching load than British teachers (Leung 1995).

## Teachers and teaching: what went wrong?

What has gone wrong? Why does Britain, a world-class power, have such relatively poor results in international comparisons of achievement? Some of the possible issues to do with teachers and teaching are considered.

### Subject knowledge

In order to train to be a teacher the minimum requirement for mathematics is a grade C at GCSE. This contrasts strongly with requirements in those countries where test results are much better than in Britain. For example, in Japan, all teachers study mathematics to the age of 18, and their level of mathematical competence (knowledge, understanding and use of mathematics) is likely to be higher than generally to be found in Britain (Whitburn 1995). Similarly, in Hungary, students must have high entry qualifications, including the equivalent of

A level mathematics (Reynolds 1996). In other Pacific Rim societies, such as Korea and Taiwan, students are recruited to teacher training with similar levels of achievements to those undertaking other courses in higher education; teaching has a much higher status than in Britain, and for clever students from poorer, rural homes it offers the opportunity for upward social mobility (Reynolds 1996).

Students on teacher training courses often exhibited great fear of mathematics. They described school mathematics as 'horrific', 'hated it', 'you didn't know what you were doing, you just knew if you got it right', and sometimes described teachers who terrified their pupils and did not offer appropriate help, rather intimidation or sarcastic comments, when pupils did not understand the concepts being taught. These experiences engendered feelings of failure and poor self-confidence in their mathematics ability (Sawyer 1993; Brown *et al.* 1999). During their teacher training course many students improved in their levels of competence, and thus their self-confidence also improved. However, during school experience students often met teachers who had poor levels of subject knowledge in mathematics and were likely to be supervised by a college tutor with no specialist mathematics knowledge; this led to the main input for mathematics while on school experience being pedagogical in nature, with help for class organisation and management, but not for the understanding of the concepts being taught (Brown *et al.* 1999).

The fear of mathematics among student teachers, their standards of subject knowledge and the need to improve these were brought to a head during 1998–9, with the government's introduction of Standards (DfEE 1998c) which students in training must achieve by the end of their teacher training course. Students at University College Worcester, as at other institutions providing courses of Initial Teacher Training (ITT), were required to undertake an audit of mathematical knowledge and then to remediate areas of weakness. Many students reported how terrifying they considered this, but as time went on, and as, at the suggestion of tutors, they set up self-help groups, used study guides, and attended remedial workshops, so their subject knowledge improved. They were asked to keep a profile of improvement, and tutors noted how students' performance in taught mathematics sessions improved, and how there was an improvement in attitude as aptitude improved. Similarly, mathematics leaders in primary schools were asked to ensure that teachers in Key Stage 2 in schools carried out an audit of their subject knowledge for mathematics, and then to provide remedial help where necessary. The effectiveness of the measures taken to ensure that all newly qualified teachers (NQTs) have reached the standards required in mathematics remains to be seen in practice. Similarly, whether the audits were undertaken in school and whether the remedial help has been undertaken, and its effectiveness, is not yet documented.

## Topic work

Teachers already in post similarly had, in the main, competence in pedagogical skills of classroom organisation and management, but often had poorly-developed mathematical knowledge, skills and understanding. One traditional teaching approach, prior to the introduction of the National Curriculum, was that of topic work, and schools' planning would centre around a theme and include elements of many subject disciplines, including mathematics. Teachers argued that this approach to curriculum design led to initial planning which took account of the children's needs (Sawyer 1993). In practice there were strong arguments that this did not really occur, that the topic and its potential became more important than the children's needs, and that this approach hid teachers' poor levels of competence in mathematics; the publication of the Alexander *et al.'s* discussion paper, Curriculum Organisation and Classroom Practice in Primary Schools, (1992), and the ensuing discussion, saw the beginning of the end of the topic approach in primary schools.

## Using published schemes

Another approach, which has survived to the present, is that of using a published scheme. Here schools buy into the planning undertaken by others. There are teaching materials, with lessons ready prepared, pupil activity and written materials, and, more lately, assessment materials. School textbooks for mathematics were available during the nineteenth century; however, in 1964, the 'Nuffield Mathematics 5 to 13' Project was launched, and teachers, books were published which explained the basic ideas underpinning mathematics learning. Eventually the pressure from schools for materials to use in the classroom led to the production of the Nuffield Mathematics Scheme in 1979, with pupil and teacher materials. Another scheme produced which also provided materials for teachers and pupils was 'Mathematics for Schools' written by Harold Fletcher in 1970 (Thompson 1997). Others followed, and today there is a plethora of published scheme material from which schools can choose. These range from the published schemes which encourage teachers to begin at the beginning of the relevant set of materials, and to work through, page by page. These materials take control of the learning, rather than the teacher making decisions about what is appropriate for the pupils. Other schemes, published in the 1990s, are organised differently, and do encourage teachers to make planning decisions, choose appropriate teaching activities, then use the pupil materials as reinforcement, practice or assessment. However, in order to use the materials in this way, teachers need to feel confident in the decisions that they make, and to have appropriate subject knowledge to underpin their teaching.

Using a scheme was 'safe'. Teachers' own levels of competence could remain hidden through the use of the scheme because the planning was already done. This hid the need for individual teachers, development of their subject knowledge (Millett and Johnson 1996). In the worst cases, there was no formal teaching; instead teachers provided workbooks or textbooks and pupils worked through these at their own rate, learning from the examples in the book. The teacher reacted to children's needs through marking of work done. There was little use made of the teacher's handbook, which provided teacher-led activities, to help with developing children's understanding. It was (and still is, in some schools) an inefficient and ineffective way of teaching (Sawyer 1993).

## Classroom pedagogy

As has already been suggested, in many classrooms active teaching did not take place. Instead children worked individually, often sitting around a table, each undertaking his or her own tasks. The teacher interacted individually with each child. Galton and Patrick (1990) found that 40 per cent of such interactions lasted for less than five seconds and Galton *et al.* (1999) suggest that in a class of 35 pupils each child could receive 6 minutes of individual interaction each day. Galton *et al.* (1999) noted that there has been a shift in practice towards whole-class teaching, probably as a result of the debate about classroom pedagogy begun by Alexander *et al.* (1992). Today's teacher is more likely to have moved towards some whole-class teaching, and that this shift can be seen in terms of 'talking at pupils through statements and not in talking *with* pupils by asking questions' (Galton *et al.* 1999). This can be summarised as shown in Figure 2.2.

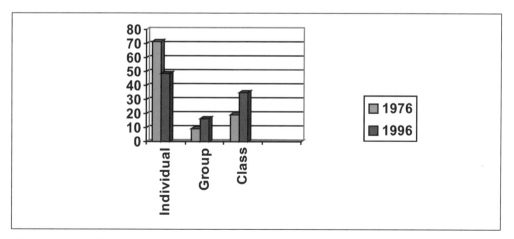

**Figure 2.2**   Changes in teacher–pupil interactions from 1976 to 1999 (from Galton *et al.* 1999)

In mathematics, this teaching style is firmly linked to the use of published schemes where teachers do not take control of the learning, as described above. Where teachers talk, children listen; there is little interaction between teachers and pupils. Questions asked usually require pupils to recall facts or solve problems, giving just one correct answer rather than speculating (Galton *et al.* 1999).

## Information and Communications Technology and Calculators

Computers were introduced into schools through government initiative in the early 1980s, but there was little software available and in many classrooms the computer was unused, 'birdcaged' (covered with a cloth). The introduction of the calculator into schools was more successful, partly because they were cheap, and so much more accessible. However, how calculators were to be used within the classroom was misunderstood by politicians, parents, and by schools. The PrIME Project (Shuard 1991), noted that children certainly still needed to learn their tables, as mental calculations were considered essential. The Calculator Aware Number Project (CAN) ran from 1986 to 1992. Teachers were asked to develop mental methods alongside the use of the calculator, rather than teaching standard algorithms (Duffin 1997). In the classroom there was much discussion about methods used and their effectiveness, which encouraged many teachers to really listen to children's explanations. Within the classrooms involved in the CAN project there were considerable advantages in this way of working, as teachers developed their skills of encouraging children to work collaboratively, and to share their work, discussing with each other and their teacher. Test comparisons between CAN and non-CAN children showed that the CAN children mainly matched or outperformed the others. However, there was a view, shared by the public and government, that calculators had replaced mental calculations, so that for pupils at school during the late 1980s and early 1990s there was an over-reliance upon the use of the calculator, to the detriment of their ability to work mentally. Research carried out since (Ruthven *et al.* 1997), concluded that 'there was no long-term influence, for better or worse, on pupils' mathematical attainment, on their achievement of number concepts, or on their attitudes to number work and calculation, as a result of their following a calculator-aware number curriculum.' The researchers found that there was a short-term improvement in attainment at Key Stage 1, but that this was no longer in evidence at Key Stage 2, perhaps because of a greater emphasis upon mental calculation.

Ruthven and Chaplin (1997) found that when Year 6 pupils used the calculator for carrying out more complex division there were difficulties, particularly in relation to how the calculator presented the answer. Pupils had normally met division with a remainder, whereas the calculator presented the answer with, in some cases many decimal digits, pupils' experience had been of decimals with money or measures, with one or two decimal digits. The most productive outcomes were where pupils used the calculator to make trial and improvements in finding solutions. The researchers concluded that the use of calculators and the concepts underlying their use needed to be actively supported in the classroom. Evidence from OFSTED (cited Ruthven *et al.* 1997) suggested that calculators were most unlikely to harm mathematical achievement, and that calculators were not overused in schools; rather the teaching of their proper use was not covered sufficiently by teachers.

## The National Curriculum

The National Curriculum, Mathematics, was introduced in 1989 for Year 1 pupils. There were 14 Attainment Targets, which set out the learning requirements for all pupils in Key Stages 1, 2, 3 and 4, with ten levels of progression. Pupils were formally assessed at the end of each key stage, with Key Stages 1–3 SATS, and Key Stage 4, GCSE papers. Teachers were required to implement the National Curriculum for mathematics, teach the programmes of study, which defined what must be taught in order to achieve the learning outcomes described in the Attainment Target Statements of Attainment (SoA). This was a criterion-referenced system, with results for individual schools to be published nationally, apart from those at Key Stage 1. Teachers were expected to assess each Statement of Attainment and to keep comprehensive records of attainment for each pupil. At the end of each key stage, using their assessment records, teachers decided upon a Teacher Assessment level of attainment for each child. This was compared with the outcomes of the Standard Assessment Task (SAT) results.

It soon became apparent that there were too many Attainment Targets for the GCSE boards to assess effectively and for the SATs to cover, even with a sampling process. The 1991 revision reduced the number of Attainment Targets to five, as shown in Figure 2.3. Whilst the number of Attainment Targets was seen to be reduced, this did not reduce the assessment workload on teachers, as the changes were mainly cosmetic, with half the number of Statements of Attainment in the 1991 version compared with the 1988 version, but each one being much broader.

A further revision, in 1995, changed the nature of the Mathematics curriculum again. This time there were programmes of study for Using and Applying Mathematics, Number, Algebra, Shape, Space and Measures, and Handling Data. Each Attainment Target consisted of a series of level descriptors, which described what pupils at that level should be able to do. The level descriptors were 'best fit'; that is, teachers decided towards the end of the Key Stage which of these was the best fit to describe a specific pupil's attainment.

For each of the 1988, 1991 and 1995 National Curricula, there were hard-fought battles for the content. Instead of a curriculum arrived at through

| Attainment Targets in the National Curriculum for Mathematics 1988 | Attainment Targets in the National Curriculum for Mathematics 1991 |
|---|---|
| Using and applying mathematics in number, algebra and measures | Using and Applying Mathematics |
| Number and number notation | Number |
| Number operations | Algebra |
| Estimation and approximation | Shape and Space |
| Patterns and generalisations | Handling Data |
| Functions, formulae and equations | |
| Graphical representation | |
| Estimation and measurement | |
| Using and applying mathematics in shape and space and handling data | |
| Properties of shapes | |
| Location and transformation | |
| Collect, record and process data | |
| Represent and interpret data | |
| Estimate and calculate probabilities | |

**Figure 2.3** Comparison of the number of Attainment Targets in the 1988 version of the National Curriculum with the 1991 version

consensus, there was intervention from government, with ill-planned and hastily-conceived ideas becoming what teachers must, by law, teach (Brown 1996). From the teachers' perspective they lost control of what happened in their classrooms; they had a curriculum which they must, by law, teach and assess attainment. Training was limited to the legal demands of what to teach and the assessment requirements. There was little or no training in subject knowledge for mathematics to help teachers to implement the curriculum.

## Teaching styles before the introduction of the National Numeracy Strategy

During the 1970s and 1980s the theories of how children learn were very much bound up in constructivism, where pupils were regarded as 'constructors' of their own knowledge and understanding of their world. New knowledge, to be useful, must link with what was already learnt (schemas), suggesting that each individual's learning would be different. These views grew from the work of Dewey and Piaget (Gipps *et al.* 1999). However, teachers operating an individualised learning system within their classroom will have little interaction with each individual child, and little active teaching will take place (Galton 1989). Where an individualised learning system is used, this is almost always accompanied by the use of published materials, where the programme of learning, and its hierarchy is set by the ordering of the topics. The responsibility for learning is transferred to the pupils and the materials, as the teacher has so little time with each child, and, instead deals with marking and helping children who are 'stuck' (Brophy 1986).

Recent research (Boaler 1998, 1999) compared the traditional, textbook method of teaching in ability sets with that of an open, project-based method in mixed ability groups, in secondary schools. The findings showed that the traditional method developed pupils with mathematical knowledge that was of limited use to them in anything other than textbook-type situations. The more progressive approach resulted in pupils who formed generalisations and were able to use their knowledge in a range of situations. Boaler suggests that 'to increase the *formalisation of the way mathematics is taught* may decrease the capability of students in real world situations'.

Descriptions of American mathematics classrooms in the mid 1980s still have a familiar ring to them in 1999. These classrooms were categorised by:

- teachers teaching in the same way that they were taught at school;
- the use of published materials as the main form of teaching new concepts;
- extensive teacher-directed explanation and questioning followed by pencil and paper tasks;
- the teacher-held view that there is a lot to teach, so that mathematics is divorced from other subjects, and separated into components such as arithmetic, geometry, etc., and further fragmentation of each component of mathematics into topics (for example, developing counting skills from 1 to 10; then to 20; then …) and that the links between areas of mathematics are not made;
- pupils absorb knowledge, rather than engaging in problem-solving where they can use and develop understanding of new knowledge.

(Romberg and Carpenter 1986)

There is much evidence (Romberg and Carpenter 1986, Aubrey 1993 and 1997) that teachers of reception children take little notice of what children already know in mathematics, and their informal methods of calculating. Instead, teachers have tended to impart a body of mathematical knowledge to reception children, regardless of their need. While the assessment process introduced with the National Curriculum has required teachers to take account of children's prior knowledge, skills and understanding on transfer from class to class and from each tier of schooling, it was not until September 1998 that all schools were required to undertake 'Baseline assessment' shortly after children entered primary school. This may account for the lack of awareness of children's prior knowledge and skills on entry to school.

In recent years, especially since the Alexander, Rose and Woodhead (1992) discussion paper, teachers have been besieged with advice on how to teach, with a strong emphasis upon teaching named, timetabled subjects, rather than teaching through topics, and with more emphasis upon whole-class teaching, which is seen as a more efficient use of teachers' time. Boaler (1998, 1999) showed in her research that the school which adopted a more progressive approach to mathematics teaching, and produced pupils who were more able to respond effectively in real-world mathematical situations, returned to traditional textbook teaching because staff were concerned about the outcome of a forthcoming OFTSTED inspection, and because of pressure from parents who wanted their children to receive traditional mathematics teaching. Responses to this included setting in primary schools; while many schools introduced this for Years 5 and 6, there are informal reports of children as young as Year 1 being set for mathematics.

Questions to primary teachers about their reasons for introducing streaming have elicited the following responses (from author questioning of teachers attending in-service training for mathematics).

### Teacher confidence with mathematics

- The more effective teacher of mathematics teaches the more able Year 5 and 6 pupils. This teacher has stronger subject knowledge in mathematics than colleagues.

### Publishing of results

- The more able children have the opportunity to perform better in SAT tests, and this enhances the school's performance in published results.
- Better SAT performance enhances the school's image; parents make choices about schools dependent upon SAT results.

### Perceived benefits to pupils

- The less able pupils are placed in a smaller group so that they can receive more effective help.
- All the children in the set are of the same sort of ability so that they do not worry so much about how the more able children are performing.

### Perceived benefits to teachers

- There is no need to differentiate the teaching as the ability within the class is so similar.
- The head (or non-teaching deputy) takes one of the sets, so that we all teach fewer children in our group.

### School policy

- We do as we're told. We don't like setting, but that is what the senior management team says we must do.

- We discussed setting at staff meetings, and decided that it would make best use of our mathematics coordinator's time if he or she took the more able sets in Key Stage 2.

These responses raise some issues:

- The more able pupils seem to be taught by the more able mathematician. The less confident teacher does not appear to receive or want to improve their subject knowledge and skills in order to manage the learning of the more able pupils. This has ramifications for younger children as their teachers need the subject knowledge to underpin their teaching.
- The need that schools have to perform well in SATs when compared with other local schools is a legacy from Thatcherism and the notion that schools are businesses in competition with each other. There is a risk that schools will concentrate their teaching to ensure that those children who are likely to be borderline level 3/4 receive more advantageous teaching than others in order to boost the number of pupils reaching the national average level at the end of Key Stage 2.
- Streaming or setting children removes from each set the range of ability, so that the less able in mathematics does not hear the explanations of their more able peers, nor appreciate what can be achieved and striven for.
- Within each set there is likely to be a wide range of needs and abilities. The children are not 'the same'. If there is no differentiation to take account of needs and the work is planned to meet the 'average' of the set, then the more able within the set may become bored, or the less able struggle to cope with the work.
- In some schools the rate of change in educational policy has been so fast that teachers have come to accept that whatever they are asked to do they will carry out.

Comparisons between setting and mixed ability teaching were made by Linchevski and Kutscher (1998) for junior high school pupils (equivalent to Years 7 and 8). The results showed that the average and weaker students in mixed ability groupings made considerable gains in achievement, and that there was a negligible loss of achievement in the more able pupils. They believed that it was possible for pupils of all abilities to learn together, and that teachers found this a satisfying teaching method. Results from research by Fuchs *et al.* (1998) showed that where pairs of high achieving pupils worked together in a mixed ability class, they produced better quality work, and as they 'worked more collaboratively and with greater cognitive conflict and resolution, focus on interacting and helpfulness and cooperation, high achievers also generated better mathematical performances with their high-achieving classmates than with their low-achieving peers.'

## Effective teaching of mathematics

Evidence from research in the 1980s suggests that there are major factors which must be addressed in order to ensure high standards of attainment in mathematics. These factors are:

- Teachers need to know what to teach and how to teach it effectively by moving through an effective sequencing of concepts and skills.
- Effective learning requires proactive, direct instruction linked to prescribed objectives. It is suggested that this cannot be taught through individualised learning procedures because these are not productive with classes of thirty.
- Teachers need effective teaching methods for working with the whole class and groups.

(Brophy 1986)

Philipp *et al.* (1994) reported that the 'extraordinary teachers' of mathematics (they were recognised by colleagues as being extremely effective in teaching) had common features:

- They were all strongly influenced by in-service and professional development programmes which encouraged deep reflection upon their practice.
- Their mathematical content knowledge was inextricably interwoven with their teaching practice. When learning new mathematical knowledge, they did so with their pupils' needs in mind.
- A belief in the need to understand the concept. Not just to be able to perform the algorithm.
- They saw learning about mathematics as understanding and recognising connections between mathematical topics. Conceptual understanding was of primary importance in their teaching.

What, then, is needed in order to be effective?

### Whole-class teaching

Throughout the 1990s there has been a push towards whole-class teaching. This is seen by the government as the answer to raising standards of attainment in mathematics, because it is believed that teachers' time will be more effectively used in teaching all of the children, rather than concentrating on small groups or individuals.

Whole-class teaching can be one of two types:

- Interactive, with all children involved, where teachers encourage quality learning.

- Transmission, where the teacher gives his or her knowledge, and children take no active part other than answering questions, which are often of the closed, recall of knowledge type. This is the traditional model of whole-class teaching.

In 1979 Good and Grouws (in Brophy and Good 1986) suggested the following overview of a model lesson involving the whole class:

- Daily review of homework: 8 minutes.
- Development: about 20 minutes of interactive whole-class teaching.
- Practice: about 15 minutes of paper based tasks.
- Setting of homework.
- Weekly review: checking of knowledge of skills and concepts covered during the previous week.
- Monthly review: checking of knowledge skills and concepts covered during the previous four weeks.

This model of teaching encouraged whole-class interaction, rather than the traditional transmission model of whole-class teaching. Regular mental work was included, which allowed for the integration of mathematical topics. Brophy and Good reported that there were considerable gains in achievement from the use of this model.

## The Barking and Dagenham experiment

Beginning in 1994 (Luxton and Last 1998), over 50 teachers from the London Borough of Barking and Dagenham visited Switzerland and Germany for a week to observe teaching methods and to consider why there is less underachievement in continental schools than in Britain and that the standards of achievement are higher in Switzerland and Germany than here in Britain. The results of the visits led to the following ten-point specification of what leads to good standards of achievement in Switzerland and Germany:

1. The teacher's aim is to ensure that virtually all the pupils reach the basic standard for the year. Teachers and pupils work together to achieve this. 'Catching up' is important.
2. A structured curriculum which emphasises consolidation, especially in number, leading to about 3 to 5 times as much time spent on practice and consolidation as is spent on the introduction of new concepts.
3. Mental work for younger children (up to about aged nine) is given absolute precedence over written methods, with number facts learnt by heart. Formal written algorithms are introduced much later. Mental calculation strategies are formally taught, rather than encouraging 'own methods'. Calculators are

regarded as potentially damaging the development of mental strategies and are not used in the primary classroom.

4. Teachers' materials, with carefully graded progression, are used. Pupils' textbooks are written with whole-class teaching in mind.

5. Whole-class teaching of number is central. Lessons are consistent in structure and last for 45 minutes.

6. There is high-quality discussion involving the whole class. There is relatively little individual writing during lessons. Pupils are encouraged from kindergarten to make oral contributions, so that they are more used to speaking to the whole class, and mistakes are used as an opportunity for all to learn. The classroom is set up in a horseshoe arrangement.

7. Individual pupils are encouraged to come to the front to lead the lesson, often with the aid of an overhead projector. Children use mathematical language correctly when explaining what they have done to others.

8. Accuracy, working, and neat, tidy layout is demanded of written work.

9. A plenary to each lesson is held, where specific ideas are reinforced which are to be learned.

10. Homework is given as a separate task for consolidation.

From this specification a model lesson outline was drawn up which consists of:

- Starter: 5 minutes mental activity.
- Main activity: 20 minutes, where a new concept is introduced or consolidated.
- Practice and Consolidation: 15 minutes, involving a written task.
- Conclusion: 5 minutes, where the main learning points of the lesson are revised.

Luxton and Last (1997 and 1998) reported that great advances were made in attainment in mental calculations; that the long tail of low achievers diminished; and that there was a new enthusiasm for number work. What they make clear in their work is that this method is not the traditional, rote-learning long associated with whole-class teaching. Rather, pupils are encouraged to take part, work together as a class, and ensure that every pupil reaches the minimum standard for the class. They advocate the use of differentiated oral questioning, so that the less able can take part and the more able are challenged.

### High achievers

It can be argued that whole-class teaching can have a detrimental effect upon the mathematical high achiever, as they may become bored with work that does not challenge them sufficiently. Luxton and Last (1998) argue that in interactive whole-class teaching the more able can have extension and enhancement activities, with oral questions specifically directed to their needs; they state that there is no evidence from Swiss and German teaching that higher achievers are held back by this teaching method.

However, there is evidence from Mills *et al.* (1994) that, for mathematically-gifted pupils there are real advantages in providing an individualised learning paced programme, where pupils are academically challenged by the topics that they study. These programmes take account of individual achievements, learning rates, and allow the high achievers to continue to learn at their own rate and with appropriate topics.

During the summer of 1999 some schools ran mathematics summer schools to try to raise the standard of achievement of those with borderline SAT scores (Level 3/4 border) before these children began their secondary education. How long will it be before similar summer schools are offered for our most able children in order to encourage their full potential?

## Low achievers

It has been argued (Luxton and Last 1998) that the low achieving pupils benefit from being taught by interactive whole-class teaching methods, as the teacher and pupils aim together for all pupils to achieve the basic learning objectives for their year. On the other hand, Prais and Luxton (1998), in arguing against the grouping suggestions with the National Numeracy Strategy, argue that the lower attainers receive 'an insufficiency of teacher's time and attention, lack of appropriate teaching material, [have] a lower capacity ... to learn on their own and lack opportunity to learn from the approaches of faster neighbouring pupils.' DfEE (1998c) suggests that through part of the daily lesson being differentiated the needs of the lower attainers will be met, and will allow them to progress at the required rate to achieve the objectives for their year.

## Developing mathematical thinking

If children are to become mathematical thinkers then they need a mathematical language in which to express their ideas. Pupils will take part in lessons in different ways: some will offer ideas, some will ask questions; others will listen but not speak; a small minority will concentrate for very short periods of time, so are likely to miss important discussions and explanations. There are three important skills which teachers need to develop if they are to help children to become mathematical thinkers. These are:

- Questioning: questions can be closed: what is 356 add 244?; or open: how many different ways can you find to add two numbers to make 600? Galton *et al.* (1999) noted that teachers have changed the proportion of their types of questions during the last 20 years. With the shift towards more whole-class teaching Galton *et al.* noted more task questions than on-task supervision, but also noted that factual and closed questions still dominated. (This study considered the whole curriculum rather than just mathematics.) Open questions encourage thinking, because these questions do not have just one 'right' answer, but there will be a range of possible responses. Such questioning, with further encouragements for thinking where children are asked 'Can you explain why that fits?…How did you work that out? … Are there other possible solutions?…' encourages a classroom climate of enquiry, where children must engage in thinking in order to respond to their teacher's questions. Comparisons between American, Japanese and Chinese children and the types of questions their teachers asked (where open questions were seen as higher level questioning) led the researchers (Perry *et al.* 1993) to conclude 'Asking higher level questions may lead to the formation of the relatively rich and broad conceptual knowledge about mathematics developed by Asian children'. Figure 2.4 shows the variety of question types which teachers asked of their pupils.

- Developing mathematical vocabulary: In order to be able to respond appropriately to questions, children need a language. In order to understand new concepts and to begin to use them in realistic situations, children need the appropriate mathematical language in order to communicate their ideas. There are concerns from some researchers, such as Zack (1999), that the expression of formal mathematical ideas in formal mathematical language can alienate the learner; however, without the appropriate language, how can children express their ideas?

- Encouraging mathematical discussion: The Open University developed the Do Talk Record process to show how important the discussion of ideas is in developing mathematical thinking. Discussion helps children to think about what they have done, identify issues and set new questions to ask themselves in order to resolve these. The emphasis upon recording enables children to develop another medium of communication, through the use of words and numbers, and numbers and symbols. One of the skills that teachers need in encouraging discussion is that of listening to pupils' replies. In listening to pupils, teachers can challenge their own mathematical thinking (Nicol 1999), especially if pupils give an unusual or complex response to a question. Another skill which teachers need is that of responding appropriately to pupils' ideas in order to extend thinking.

- Solving problems: Mathematics must be a useful tool for children. Solving contextual problems, or investigations, enables children to choose then use their mathematics. Newstead (1998) showed that children who were involved in problem-solving activities where teachers encouraged the discussion of pupils' strategies showed less mathematical anxiety than pupils who were taught by more traditional methods.

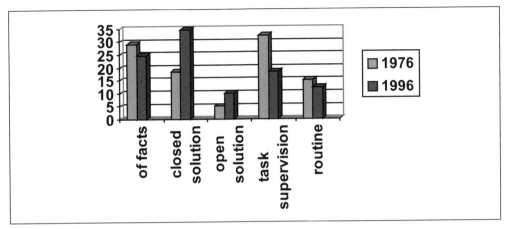

**Figure 2.4**    The nature of teachers' questions (from Galton *et al.* 1999)

## Differentiation

Traditionally, through the use of published mathematics schemes, teachers have differentiated by either having pupils working individually through the scheme, or by selecting work from the scheme at an appropriate level for attainment groups. Rigid adherence to the scheme did not ensure that all pupils attained appropriate levels, as the scheme was restrictive in its approach (Millett and Johnson 1996). In recent years, as mentioned previously, some primary schools have introduced setting into ability groups as a means of differentiation. The trials of the National Numeracy Project (DfEE 1998d) showed that with the concentration upon whole-class, interactive teaching, differentation during part of the lesson is an effective means of ensuring that the range of needs are met. The recommendation of up to four ability groups within the class makes this manageable.

Differentiation can be by:

- differentiated questioning;
- providing group, paired or individual work suited to the ability of the pupil;
- offering support from a classroom assistant;
- providing modified learning materials, such as taped questions rather than written, for those with specific needs.

## Grouping

When working away from the teacher, how to group the pupils is a major consideration. Teachers have tried various groupings during the last 30 years, including those of friendship, ability, age, and mixed ability, as well as pairs and working individually. Such groupings need to be chosen according to the nature of the task, rather than a specific grouping always being used. Studies have shown

(Nattiv 1994) that where pupils work in cooperative groups, and are taught 'helping behaviours', there was a gain in attainment where pupils gave explanations, received explanations from others, and gave and received help. There was no improvement where pupils received no help after requesting it. Grouping must be suited to a purpose. For example, asking pairs to work together to play a mathematical game and to record their results will encourage them to discuss as they work, so that they have opportunities to use mathematical vocabulary. Where there is a written exercise to be worked through, individual working for 10 to 15 minutes would be appropriate. At other times, pupils may need to work in cooperative groups in order to carry out a task which is appropriate for a group to engage in, such as a number game, or a practical measures activity.

## Gender

The differences in performance between genders noted in Cockcroft (1982) appear to have been addressed by teachers. McCaslin *et al.* (1994) observed American primary pupils who, after a whole-class input by their teacher on perimeter and, later, area, worked in small groups. They were questioned with regard to their attitudes to learning, and it was noted that:

- The interpersonal experiences which pupils experienced in small groups did not necessarily affect their learning.
- For some pupils, working in small groups was stressful because they found the interpersonal experiences difficult. These pupils were more likely to benefit if they remembered that when feeling stressed about their work they reconsidered the task or sought help.
- Gender was not a driving theme in the pupils' small-group experiences. Achievement was not differentiated by gender, nor did the pupils comment on stereotypical gender behaviour. The classroom expectations in terms of gender issues were reflected in the small group behaviour.
- Mixed gender groups could have a positive effect upon pupil engagement with the task. It was considered that this might well be a developmental feature as pupils began to move away from insistence upon working in same-gender groups. Initially more shy, pupils began to be intellectually stimulated by being in a mixed gender group.

HMI (1998) referred to the improvements in mathematical attainment made by a sample of pupils in the first cohort of the National Numeracy Project trial. Boys in Years 3 and 4 started with achievement behind girls, and overtook the girls in just five terms. In Year 6, the girls started behind the boys and within the five terms achieved similar scores to the boys. Overall, the results for girls and boys were similar, which does suggest that teachers are more aware today of using appropriate learning styles to meet the needs of both boys and girls.

## Race and bilingualism

More than half the world's population regularly uses more than one language (Emblen 1996). In many schools in Britain today, there are pupils whose home language is not English, and thus they do not learn about mathematics in their first language. Some children may well have experienced racism, which may undermine their self-esteem and thus their ability to achieve in mathematics. In some schools pupils' ethnicity is responded to positively, with the setting up of, for example, number systems from around the world, numbers written and spoken in home languages. This does much to raise pupils' self-esteem as they perceive that the school values their home language (Emblen 1996). However, in many areas there is little support for bilingual teaching within the classroom, and so pupils may well learn about mathematics as they learn to speak English. This has ramifications for how teachers communicate ideas and understand their pupils' responses.

Pupils need to talk about their mathematics in order to facilitate their learning. Through using new vocabulary, trying it out in their thinking and speaking, it becomes familiar and meaningful. As Rowland (1995) noted, there is a distinction between 'talking mathematics' and 'talking about mathematics'. For the bilingual child, who has limited English, but good command of their home language, this can present problems. Fillmore and Valadez (1986) referred to the limited set of vocabulary items which pupils need to learn, and that these are then used in problems to be solved, where everyday English is used too. Often, such word problems do not make it explicit which operation is needed; this is to be inferred from the subject matter of the problem.

HMI (1998) noted in their report that in the National Numeracy Project trial pupils for whom English was an additional language, and who were just becoming familiar with English, made relatively better progress and began to catch up with those for whom English is their first language. This may be because of the interactive teaching style, with whole-class questioning and responding, so that all hear the mathematical and everyday English vocabularies used correctly.

## Teaching for understanding

To be effective as a teacher of mathematics, there are underlying values and beliefs which teachers need to consider. These include:

- How teachers view mathematics: if it is a set of procedures to be mastered then the traditional transition method would be appropriate. If, however, it is a conceptual tool for understanding situations and solving problems, then this is more consistent with a view of learning where pupils learn through constructing knowledge (Putnam *et al.* 1992). An interactive teaching style is more likely than the transmission model to lead to children building schemas as they will be encouraged to discuss, compare methods, understand how and why aspects of mathematics 'work'.

- Teachers' own subject knowledge: where this is strong, and teachers understand the underlying concepts, then pupils are more likely to receive good quality teaching. However, findings from research by Askew *et al.* (1997) suggest that a qualification such as A level in mathematics or a mathematics degree will not necessarily make them better teachers. The reasons for this may be to do with the higher levels of mathematics seeming unconnected with what they were asked to teach at primary level.

- Teachers' beliefs about what it means to be numerate: Askew *et al.* (1997) identified three different orientations amongst teachers of primary aged pupils. These are:

  - Connectionist orientation: these teachers believe that being numerate involves using calculation methods which are both efficient and effective; having confidence and ability in mental methods; being able to select a method of calculation based on the operation and numbers involved; aware of the links between different aspects of the mathematical curriculum; and being able to reason, justify and eventually prove results about number.

  - Transmission orientation: these teachers believe that being numerate involves having the ability to perform standard procedures or routines; a heavy reliance upon paper and pencil methods; the selection of a method of calculation primarily on the basis of the operation involved; having confidence in separate aspects of the mathematics curriculum; and being able to identify the particular routine or technique required to solve context problems.

  - Discovery orientation: these teachers believe that being numerate involves finding the answer to a calculation by any method; having a heavy reliance on practical methods; the selection of a method of calculation primarily on the basis of the operation involved; having confidence in separate aspects of the mathematics curriculum; and being able to use and apply mathematics using practical apparatus.

- Teachers beliefs about how pupils become numerate: again, from Askew *et al.* (1997) come the following models of beliefs:

  - Connectionist orientation: pupils become numerate through purposeful interpersonal activity based on interactions with others; they learn through being challenged and struggling to overcome difficulties; most pupils are able to become numerate; they have strategies for calculating but the teacher has responsibility for helping them refine their methods; and pupil misunderstandings need to be recognised, made explicit and worked on.

- Transmission model: pupils become numerate through individual activity based on following instructions; they learn through being introduced to one mathematical routine at a time and remembering it; they vary in their ability to become numerate; their strategies for calculating are of little importance, and they need to be taught standard procedures; and their misunderstandings are the result of failure to grasp what has been taught and need to be remediated by further reinforcement of the 'correct' method.

- Discovery orientation: pupils become numerate through individual activity based on actions on objects; they need to be 'ready' before they can learn certain mathematical ideas; they vary in their rate at which their numeracy develops; their own strategies are the most important and understanding is based upon working things out yourself; and pupil misunderstandings are the result of pupils not being 'ready' to learn the ideas.

• Teachers' beliefs about how best to teach pupils to become numerate: Askew *et al.* (1997) identified:

- Connectionist orientation: teaching and learning are seen as complementary; numeracy teaching is based upon *dialogue* between teacher and pupils to explore understandings; learning about mathematical concepts and the ability to apply these are learned alongside each other; connections between mathematical ideas needs to be acknowledged in teaching; and application is best approached through challenges that need to be reasoned through.

- Transmission orientation: teaching is seen as separate from and having priority over learning; numeracy teaching is based on *verbal explanations* so that pupils understand teachers' methods; learning about mathematical concepts precedes the ability to apply these concepts; mathematical ideas need to be introduced in discrete packages; and application is best approached through 'word' problems which give contexts for calculating routines.

- Discovery orientation: learning is seen as separate from and having priority over teaching; numeracy teaching is based on *practical activities* so that pupils discover methods for themselves; learning about mathematical concepts precedes the ability to apply these concepts; mathematical ideas need to be introduced in discrete packages; and application is best approached through using practical equipment.

## Solving problems

The connectionist teacher described above used problem-solving as a means of encouraging pupils to understand and use their growing mathematical knowledge.

Where pupils are encouraged to solve problems they also have the opportunity to try diverse ways of solving problems and to consider appropriateness and efficiency, to discuss how they can apply their mathematical knowledge, and to explore their thinking (Good *et al.* 1992). Pupils become resourceful in their approaches to problem-solving, recognise and accept a variety of solutions and assume a shared responsibility with the teacher for their mathematical learning (Franke and Carey 1997).

Gray (1991) showed that pupils solving numerical problems used one of three general solution approaches:
1.  Immediately recalled the number fact.
2.  Deduced the solution from alternative known facts.
3.  Used a procedure with which they felt confident.

He found that the above-average pupils tended to use solution 2, whilst the lower achievers made substantial use of the procedural approach (counting), because they were much less successful at learning number bonds or using ones that they do know and so were unable to deduce unknown facts from known. Hart (1993) reported that the classroom environment has an impact upon pupils' ability to solve problems; for example, some pupils may believe that all of the numbers in a problem must be used to solve it, rather than reading and sifting the data in the problem. The wording of the problem can have impact upon pupils' ability to solve it. The following three problems can all be solved by subtracting 5 from 8, but in tests pupils found 1 easiest, then 2 and then 3. The wording of the problem affected the pupils' ability to abstract appropriate mathematics from it.
1.  'Joe had 8 marbles; then he gave 5 marbles to Tom; how many marbles does Joe have now?'
2.  'Joe and Tom have 8 marbles altogether; Joe has 3 marbles; how many marbles does Tom have?'
3.  'Joe had some marbles; then Tom gave him 5 more marbles; now Joe has 8 marbles; how many marbles did Joe have in the beginning?'

(Verschaffel and De Corte 1993)

Pupils taught in classes where problem-solving was central to the teaching were found to have higher levels of achievement on standardised tests and showed a belief in the importance of finding their own ways to solve problems, were task-orientated, and more likely to be motivated to try and understand (Wood and Sellers 1997).

From this evidence can be drawn some conclusions about problem-solving:

*   Pupils who learn through problem-solving are more likely to make efficient use of their mathematical knowledge constructs because they develop understanding through contextualising their mathematics, discussion of possible solutions, and comparing results and solution strategies with others.

- Pupils who learn in problem-solving classrooms are more likely to develop confidence in their mathematical knowledge and their ability to use it.
- Pupils need to have effective recall of known number facts and appropriate and effective strategies for deducing the unknown from the known.
- Pupils need to understand the problem, and to be able to abstract relevant data from the problem in order to identify appropriate solution-finding strategies.

The Numeracy Project trial emphasised the development of problem-solving skills alongside the development of concepts, understanding, mental calculation strategies and recall. The success reported by HMI in trial schools which successfully implemented the trial materials (HMI 1998) suggests that the development of problem-solving skills alongside learning of facts is essential to understanding mathematics and being able to use it effectively.


## The National Numeracy Strategy

In September 1999 all primary schools were expected to introduce the National Numeracy Strategy and to use the National Numeracy Framework for planning teaching (DfEE 1999). Its implementation was part of the government drive to raise standards of attainment in numeracy, with targets set for 75 per cent of all 11-year-olds to achieve at least level 4 in the National Curriculum tests for mathematics by 2002. Whilst the National Numeracy Strategy does not have statutory status, schools were told 'From September 1999, schools will provide a structured daily mathematics lesson of 45 minutes to one hour for all pupils of primary age. Teachers will teach the whole class together for a high proportion of the time, and oral and mental work will feature strongly in each lesson' (DfEE,1999). The Framework provides guidance on what to teach, supplementing the National Curriculum Order for mathematics. It contains a yearly teaching programme, setting out the learning objectives to be taught for each year from Reception to Year 6 and suggestions for planning, key objectives for what must be achieved for each year, and examples which illustrate each teaching objective, a selection of what pupils should know, understand and be able to do by the end of each school year (DfEE 1999).

The Framework divides the mathematics curriculum under four headings:

- Numbers and the number system.
- Calculations.
- Solving problems.
- Measures, shape and space.

There is an emphasis upon pupils developing efficient counting skills, understanding place value and using this in estimation, approximation, and comparing and ordering numbers. Great emphasis is placed upon teaching pupils mental calculation strategies, and encouraging them to use these in problem-solving situations. Pupils are expected to develop rapid recall of addition, subtraction, multiplication and division facts, and to derive other facts from known ones, and to develop methods of checking calculations. The emphasis is upon mental calculation; standard algorithmic procedures are not taught until at least Year 4. Pupils are expected to solve problems involving real life, measures and money, and to reason and generalise about numbers and shapes. Handling data is taught, with an emphasis on problem-solving. The use of a calculator is not introduced until Year 5.

Teachers are expected to model their lessons upon the Framework structure:

- Oral and mental starter: whole-class session, based upon facts and skills already taught. Pupils respond rapidly to counting, recall, or mental calculation strategy questions, differentiated to enable all pupils in the class to take part.
- Main teaching input and pupil activity: this is intended to start as a whole-class taught session, where new concepts and skills are introduced or reinforced. The learning objectives are made quite clear to the pupils, either being written on the chalk board or being spoken. Through the use of differentiated questioning, the whole class, regardless of ability, is involved in thinking, and answering questions. Pupils are encouraged to explain their methods and their thinking. This is interactive teaching, with problem-solving used to encourage rapid recall of facts, deduction of the unknown from the known, explanations and considerations of efficiency of methods, using appropriate mathematical language and vocabulary to explain thinking, and the opportunity to learn from each other through hearing others' thinking. It is an interactive teaching session. Pupils will also spend time on activities, in groups, pairs or individually, according to the type of activity and their learning needs. These may be written tasks or games.
- Plenary: here the pupils consider what they have learnt. They will be reminded by their teacher of the main learning objectives of the lesson, and pupils may share with others the outcomes of their work.

The style of teaching is teacher and pupil active. The teaching is interactive, with questioning to encourage thinking and recall of great importance. Specific mental calculation strategies are taught; these are not left to chance. The emphasis is upon a lesson which moves at a good pace, where pupils listen and respond, and all have the opportunity to join in. Teachers are encouraged to make connections between learning so that pupils can draw upon what they already know and make sense of new knowledge and skills.

## Mental calculation strategies

This is a particular feature of the Framework. Strategies taught in Reception and Year 1 are used again and again, with larger number ranges. For example, in Year 1 pupils are taught to 'Add 9 to single digit numbers by adding 10 then subtracting 1'. Examples across the age range are:

Year 1: $6 + 9 = 6 + 10 - 1$
Year 2: $35 + 19 = 35 + 20 - 1$
Year 3: $543 + 11 = 543 + 10 + 1$
Year 4: $74 + 58 = 74 + 60 - 2$
Year 5: $274 + 96 = 274 + 100 - 4$
Year 6: $4.3 + 2.9 = 4.3 + 3 - 0.1$

Thus, a mental calculation strategy learned in Year 1 is developed over time to include using knowledge of place value and decimals.

## Recording

Until Year 4, pupils record horizontally, having used mental calculation strategies and rapid recall to find solutions. In Year 4, the standard algorithms are introduced. This is a deliberate policy, based upon evidence from European countries, that pupils need to develop their mental calculation strategies first, be efficient with those, before they learn the standard written methods.

## The place of Information Communication Technology within the Framework

The use of the calculator is delayed until Year 5. This is to enable pupils to develop effective calculation strategies, mental, paper and pencil and algorithmic methods, so that they do not become reliant upon the use of the calculator to perform operations. This is probably a response to government intervention, as there is a belief (misplaced, as already shown in this chapter) that the use of the calculator interferes with the development of sound computation skills.

There are some references to the use of the computer. At Key Stage 1 the use of a floor turtle for work on direction is included in the examples to illustrate teaching objectives. In Year 3, it is suggested that a simple graphing program can be used to enter and display data. Other examples include the use of a binary tree program to sort a set of numbers by their properties (Year 5); in Year 6 use turtle graphics to draw polygons; and for offering extension activities for those who need more challenging contexts. Inappropiate use of the computer includes individual use of computer programs during the daily lesson (except where IEPs suggest that this is necessary). Computer software should only be used in the daily mathematics lesson if it is the most efficient and effective way to meet the lesson's objectives (DfEE 1999)

CHAPTER 3

# Mathematics software and its use

*Bob Fox, Ann Montague-Smith and Sarah Wilkes*

This chapter will provide a brief survey of types of software available to support the teaching of numeracy. There are many such items in existence (of which, in perhaps most schools, few are in regular use), and any attempt to provide an exhaustive and comprehensive list here would necessarily result in no more than the briefest of descriptions for each. Inevitably, some readers may be surprised at what we have chosen to omit, but inclusion here does not imply endorsement. The intention is to give some insight into the major categories of mathematics software as we see them.

First, however, we need to elaborate a little on some points made in the opening chapter. We have said that there is a distinction to be made between ICT as a National Curriculum subject in its own right and ICT as a medium for enhancing learning and teaching across the curriculum. The two should not be mutually exclusive. Perhaps the best way to think of it is that time spent on teaching the National Curriculum subject should focus largely on developing pupils' skills and understanding of the technology, its uses and its capabilities; and pupils should also have the opportunity to put those learned and developed skills to good use in all other subjects. There is very little point in teaching children to word process for its own sake, or merely so that they can be said to know about word processing. They should learn to word process so that they can use their developed skills to enhance their capacity to write (and particularly to create and modify text, rather than merely copy up existing text) in the context of the literacy hour, or in history, or science, or whatever.

There is a problem, however. The Strategy documents for both literacy and numeracy make it quite clear that designated time is to be spent on meeting the objectives for literacy and numeracy, and not on teaching IT skills. Literacy and numeracy currently dominate the primary curriculum to the extent that in most schools they occupy virtually the whole morning every day, which means that everything else must be squeezed into the limited afternoon space, including the teaching of ICT as a discrete subject. There is every possibility that this teaching will not happen, and that teachers will be tempted to use some literacy or numeracy time to teach ICT skills, at the possible expense of using ICT as a medium for teaching and learning.

In practice, of course, the distinction is not always so clear cut. Though the principal focus of the lesson may be on numeracy, pupils using ICT will incidentally be developing their ICT skills; and it may well be the case that in order to move pupils forwards in their numeracy work, some assistance and instruction in ICT will be given. If during a mathematics lesson a child was struggling to input data into a datafile or spreadsheet, one would not decline to help on the grounds that it was not an ICT lesson. The point is that one must not lose sight of the intended outcomes of the lesson, which must be expressed in terms of numeracy (or literacy, as the case may be).

There is another dimension to this, which we need to address. We have seen that the rapid movement towards the installation of computer rooms or suites was partly in response to OFSTED's concerns about standards in ICT. There is every reason to believe that where whole classes or half-classes of children have access to machines simultaneously, rather than having to wait days or weeks for their turn, the development of children's ICT skills can proceed far more effectively than has previously been the case. The major variable in this case is often the teacher's own confidence, experience and understanding, and there has even been a move towards specialist teaching of ICT which could prove to be extremely damaging to the effective implementation of ICT in other subjects, if non-specialists thus become marginalised and deskilled. What we need to consider is whether removing all the computers from the classrooms and placing them in one room has a negative effect on the school's capacity to use ICT effectively in the teaching and learning of numeracy. If there are also computers in the classroom, all well and good, but if children need to go to the computer room every time they need to generate a graph, say, then there are extra logistical factors to consider – particularly as in most schools the numeracy time is happening in all classes simultaneously. Some schools have developed an apparently satisfactory rota system for use of the computer room during numeracy time, but this could have an inhibiting effect on numeracy planning, or, as anecdotal evidence suggests is already the case in some schools where computer rooms have recently been established, the computer room could stand idle all morning, with nobody at all using ICT during the numeracy time. We will examine this question in greater detail in Chapter 5, but for the present we will note it as a factor as we consider the uses of different categories of mathematics software.

## Functions of ICT

In the DfEE requirements for courses of Initial Teacher Training (and the intended outcomes of New Opportunities Fund training), four functions of ICT are identified, which should be considered when deciding when or when not to use ICT in subject teaching. In this chapter we will consider the extent to which they may be considered to apply to categories of mathematics software – and where they would not be particularly relevant. To justify the use of ICT, it would only be necessary to demonstrate that one of the four functions was effective. The four functions are as follows.

### Speed and automatic functions

Does the software make it possible to do things quickly which would otherwise be too time consuming, or to do things automatically which would otherwise involve, say, much tedious repetition? Examples here might be graph-drawing software, or such facilities within a database, which would greatly speed up the process of creating a graph, thus leaving more time to concentrate on interpreting the graph (McFarlane 1997). Speed is not of the essence in Logo, where it is often actually an advantage to be able to see the turtle draw the lines of a shape. Modern processors are so fast that it is necessary to slow down the drawing speed to make it acceptable.

### Capacity and range

Very few pieces of primary maths software have a specific need for enormous capacity, either of computer memory or of storage (e.g. CD–ROM), and where these facilities are utilised, it tends to be for the purpose of enhancing graphic quality rather than holding masses of data. There is a gigantic range of material on the World Wide Web, but relatively little of it relates to teaching and learning in primary mathematics, yet, at least. Probably the only mathematics software that really needs a large capacity is an Integrated Learning System (ILS), which needs to store a vast range of materials in order to cater for the individual differences of their users.

### Provisionality

Logo is a good example of provisionality. If everything one told the screen turtle to do worked perfectly first time, Logo would be very boring and largely pointless. The whole point about Logo is that you can formulate your hypothesis about how to achieve something, test it in practice, and modify your hypothesis repeatedly until you achieve what you set out to do. The computer is entirely non-judgemental, and it does not tell you that you are wrong or stupid if you are not immediately successful, but it gives you scope to be adventurous, take risks and try out ideas. At one level, most simple drill-and-practice software does not display provisionality, as for every question asked there is a preset and non-negotiable correct answer; but most such software allows you a second chance if you are not successful first time. Data handling software always has provisionality; in particular, graphing software can usually adjust the columns or calibration of the graph dynamically as you modify the data. Much effective spreadsheet work relies extensively on provisionality.

## Interactivity

This is a slightly troubling term. Mostly, in the context of computer software, we take it to mean that the way a computer responds to the user's input will depend on the nature of the input. At a simple level, a drill-and-practice program will respond differently, according to whether the response it receives is correct or not; at that level, the second little Basic program in Chapter 1 can be said to be interactive. At a more complex level, a sophisticated ILS will vary the difficulty of the questions it presents in response to the accuracy and speed of the user's responses. The reason it is troubling is that the Numeracy Strategy is closely bound up with the concept of interactive teaching, particularly of whole classes, and in that context the term implies rather more. It implies a two-way or many-way dialogue among human beings which is far more susceptible to nuance than any computer program is ever likely to be. Perhaps at root the difference is not of manner, but of degree.

## Software classification

Higgins and Muijs (1999) identify some distinct strands in mathematics software, which we will follow in this chapter. On the one hand, there are drill-and-practice programs, which are built around assumptions about learning that stem from behaviourism. Related to these in their underpinning assumptions, but functioning at a much more sophisticated level, there are Integrated Learning Systems. The software that belongs to both of these categories takes as its purpose the development of mathematical skills, and is very much concerned with the effective transmission of an existing body of knowledge. Our second little Basic program may be considered as representative of the simpler of these categories.

Another category is 'strategy development and pattern recognition' (Higgins and Muijs 1999), which contains small programs written to teach or illustrate or explore specific mathematical concepts, e.g. problem solving. In the heyday of teacher-written software for the BBC 'B' a range of programs were devised, some much better than others, and for a while they were quite well used in many primary classrooms. But they were unsophisticated in appearance, and had limited applicability, and very often teachers were not clear what they were actually supposed to do with them. Sending children away into a corner to 'play' them was not visibly rewarding, though often if the 'sound' option was turned on the 'reward' was all too obvious when the task was completed! As computers became faster and more powerful they went out of fashion. The coming of the Numeracy Strategy has given them a new lease of life, however, particularly as raw materials for teacher-led whole-class or group maths activities. The best programs have been rewritten and redesigned to take advantage of the superior facilities of modern computers. Software in this category is now variously known as 'Useful Little Programs' or 'Legacy Software', and many of the ideas explored in the following chapters of this book stem from the same thinking that has brought these programs back to prominence.

Another type of software is the adventure game where children are encouraged to take part in a story and solve problems in order to reach the conclusion of the game.

At the opposite end of the spectrum there is software that is designed to develop mathematical understanding, which is based upon constructivist principles. Specifically in this category there is Logo, which is built to reflect Piaget's view of learning. Constructivism is concerned to provide learning environments in which children can construct their own meanings. The section on Logo which follows also includes an account of floor robots, which provide a tangible alternative to screen turtles. Neither of our Basic programs as such would fit into this category, but if you made the proposed modifications to them, the act of doing so may well have demonstrated something about the constructivist view of learning, as the tasks were open-ended to an extent, and you were not told precisely how to do them.

These categories are located within specific and opposing theories of learning, but the category of software tools, which includes graphing programs, databases and spreadsheets, may be thought of as neutral, and not based on any such theory, and can be employed as the user sees fit. Our first Basic program could be considered to be a very primitive software tool.

The survey that follows is necessarily brief, and cannot say all that there is to say. You are therefore invited to consider for yourself (or discuss in a seminar, staff meeting or in-service course) the teaching and learning implications of each, bearing in mind the following:

1.  Which of the four functions of ICT described above are exhibited by this software? If none, can you justify using it?
2.  If you were to use this software, for what broad age-groups is it appropriate? Can it cater for different abilities within a single class? Within a mixed-age class?

3. Apart from the mathematical concepts in the software, what other demands does it make on the user, particularly in terms of language use, or ICT skills needed to navigate it?
4. For what sort of classroom or computer room use would it be suitable? Or does that matter? What would you need to do to maximise its use by your class? How much time would you expect to devote to it?
5. How well does the program fit in with your view of how children learn most effectively? Does it present children with learning opportunities at least as rich as those you could provide by other means?
6. What do *you* need to know in order for your children to use this software effectively?
7. Could children use this program without adult supervision? How could you monitor children's progress? What interventions would you anticipate making?
8. What would constitute evidence of success, and how would you assess and record it?
9. What would you expect children to be able to do after using this software that they could not do (or could not do as well) beforehand?
10. Can you identify outcomes from software use that match the specified *numeracy outcomes* for your children (we are not here considering ICT outcomes)?

If you are considering making use of any of the software mentioned (or any other) as a means of developing the use of ICT in your numeracy teaching, ensure that you have established satisfactory answers to all the above.

We now consider in detail these five distinct classifications of software:

- Drill and Practice
- ILS
- Maths Adventure and Problem Solving
- Logo
- Data Handling

The examples of software that follow are some of those found currently in use in schools.

## Drill and Practice software

### Background

With the introduction of the computer into the primary classroom in the early 1980s, teachers had limited choice of software for mathematics. Much of what was available was of the drill and practice type (Blows and Wray 1989). The earliest programs were practice in recall of table facts and number bonds. The software was loaded from a cassette tape; it took ages, and frequently crashed before it was loaded. Children would input their answer; the computer rewarded them with a tick, a 'happy' sound, or a moving image if the answer was correct; if it was wrong there might be a cross, an 'unhappy' sound or no moving image. The software gave the children no help if the answer was wrong. Some of this early software kept a record of the number of correct responses which the teacher could access. The noise generated by this software was at times disturbing: loud, especially software whose reinforcement for the correct answer was a firework display, for example. It was intrusive, disturbed other children working in the classroom, and could become extremely irritating (Walton 1984). However, looking back over the last 18 years, there was also a frisson of excitement about using the computer and drill and practice software. It was novel, the images did, sometimes, move on screen, and children did seem to enjoy the novelty of using such programs. (Indeed, the author remembers some children who preferred the sound produced when the answer was wrong, and would deliberately work through the questions ensuring that the answer to each one was wrong!)

Pam Linn (cited in Noss 1991) described the use of the computer in school as 'nothing but an electronic workcard, blackboard calculator or drawing block'. The notion of an 'electronic workcard' does accurately reflect drill and practice software, which provides examples for children to work through, without giving any help or advice. Its only advantage over a printed workcard is that it will give instant feedback on whether or not the answer is correct.

Since these early days of drill and practice software the technology has moved forward. Software moved from tape to disk, which was much more reliable and had more storage space so that the multimedia aspects of what was produced were more attractive (and noisy!). Today such software is produced mainly on CD–ROMs, which allows for the visual image to be much more interactive.

Today's drill and practice software, on CD–ROM, is likely to include text, audio commentary, sound effects, pictures and perhaps an animation or video clip. However, the stimulation-effect from such software is unlikely to be as marked as will be found in today's games software, which has an international market, and through which the software producers can make huge profits. Educational software in Britain has a much smaller market and is thus far less likely to have the range of features seen in good games programs (Ager 1998).

### Towards the millennium: interactive drill and practice

Today drill and practice software is interactive, with a game to be played. This can be a game played between two children both working at the computer, or one or two children playing against the computer. For most programs the children input their names before they begin to play and sometimes the program is personalised, with their names appearing in the score box on screen. Often the software will keep a score showing the number of correct responses. The following are some examples of software, chosen at random from today's software producers' catalogues.

**Sumthing** (Resource) is a currently available program, on floppy disk. It provides practice in the four rules and ordering numbers for children aged 5–8 years. Arithmetic questions are set out horizontally. The teacher or child can choose the mathematics topic to be practised and set the difficulty level. The instructions appear on screen, and are not particularly easy to follow. Only the correct answer is accepted; errors are rewarded with, for example, being 'eaten' by a creature. There is a button to click on if help is required; which responds with messages such as congratulations on achieving a zero score. No records are stored for the teacher to identify how the children performed.

   The interaction here is through new creatures appearing on screen. The rewards are successfully completing the game. However, if children produce wrong answers there are no in-built help features for them to use, and they will be thrown back on their own resources if stuck. The images are static, with a limited range of colours used. This will not appear attractive to those children used to playing games on their home computer.

**Hooray for Maths** (Lander Software), this software provides practice in the four rules of arithmetic for children aged 5–12. It is currently available on CD–ROM, which enables far more data to be stored and the use of improved graphics makes it a visually more appealing program. Arithmetic questions are set out horizontally. It is possible for the teacher or child to set the level of difficulty and there is a record which keeps the score. Within the teacher-control system it is possible to see the responses to each question the child answered; however, it is not a convenient system to use. There is on-screen response if three attempts to answer a question are made and the answer is still wrong; the response is to give the correct solution, but without any explanation.

**The Number Works** (Sherston Software), this is currently available on CD–ROM and provides practice in the operation of the four rules of arithmetic and place value. It is suitable for children aged about 7–9. It is an adventure program, where questions have just one answer, rather than problem-solving situations. Help screens are provided if children are stuck and a prompt appears to use the help if repeated wrong answers are given for the same question. The teacher can choose whether to use horizontal or vertical recording for arithmetic. However, the help screens only provide vertical examples where there are tens and units, which is not in line with the expectations of the National Numeracy Strategy, and this could be very confusing for children who have only been introduced to horizontal recording. The software keeps a log of children's results. It is also possible for the teacher to choose which activity is to be used, rather than asking children to work through the adventure game.

**Mighty Maths: Carnival Countdown** (Iona Software), this currently available software comes on CD–ROM and is suitable for Key Stage 1 and Year 3. It includes, amongst others, the topics of addition and subtraction and comparing and ordering numbers. There is good use of multimedia, with humorous screen images, spoken instructions, cartoon-like video clips and help buttons. Addition and subtraction are shown in both horizontal and vertical formats. However, the stronger image on screen is the vertical one, and this is where the answer is shown. This does not fit with the requirements of the National Numeracy Strategy for delay in the introduction of formal algorithmic methods for addition and subtraction until Year 4. A record for each child is kept, which the teacher can access.

**Mighty Maths: Number Heroes** (Iona Software), this currently available software comes on CD–ROM. It includes activities for addition, subtraction, multiplication and division, place value, number patterns (algebra), shape and space and probability. It is suitable for children in Key Stage 2 and the level of difficulty for each mathematics topic can be determined by either the teacher or the child. The children input their names when they begin their session with the software, and this is used to identify their performance in the records. For some activities an on-screen four-rule calculator, or, for fraction work, a fraction calculator, is available. If children make an error in number work they are invited to try again. For pattern and shape activities further on-screen help may be provided, usually in the form of further information.

Sometimes questions require two answers, and if only one is given this is an error and children are told to try again and to look for further answers. According to the handbook, which accompanies the software, the activities are designed to emphasise and develop problem-solving skills rather than pupils recalling memorised facts. It is intended that children talk to each other and learn from one anothers' methods of solving problems. They are expected to explain their reasoning to their teacher. However, questions do have just one answer. There is a quiz section where children choose the type of question they would like to answer, and its level of difficulty. They can either play against the computer, or against another child. Within the quiz section they can earn extra points by checking their opponent's answer. The use of multimedia is good, with moving images, cartoon-like video clips, speech, help buttons, and text on screen. The program can be noisy, but the use of headphones resolves this.

Again, addition and subtraction is set out, from tens and units on, in vertical form, and this will be confusing to children who have not met this format before, and for those who have, it may force them into solving the problem using standard algorithmic methods rather than choosing from an array of suitable mental strategies.

## Case Study 1

An urban first school had just purchased its first PC, kept in the school library. Prior to this the school had used Acorn machines and software, still in classrooms, and had a very limited range of mathematics software. For the PC, they had purchased both Carnival Countdown and Number Heroes from Iona Software. Two teachers share the coordination role for ICT; one teaches Year 1 and is also the design and technology coordinator, the other teaches Y3 and is also the mathematics coordinator. On looking at the software, which had been recommended for purchase by the LEA ICT support team, the teachers were shocked to discover that vertical forms of recording were included for Key Stage 1, and for Key Stage 2 for tens and units addition and subtraction. This was a dilemma for the school, particularly with the impending introduction of the National Numeracy Strategy and its delay in introducing formal algorithmic recording methods. The school introduced an oral and mental starter activity at the beginning of each mathematics lesson at the beginning of the academic year.

Two children at a time were asked by their teacher to work with the researcher in the library for about 15 minutes. The purpose of the observation was to note:

- How the children responded to the software.
- How they worked together.
- What strategies they used when they gave the wrong answer or were stuck.
- How the strategies that they used in oral and mental work transferred to using drill and practice software.
- What differences or similarities there were between the Year 1 and Year 3 children in their approach to using the software.

The children were chosen by their teacher for:

- being reasonably articulate;
- having reached at least an average level in mathematics within their class.

Six Year 1 children were observed, four boys and two girls, aged between $6\frac{1}{4}$ and $6\frac{3}{4}$ years. They were asked to work at an activity which involved sorting numbers as they appeared from a cave. The numbers were to be placed inside a Venn diagram, which had a ring inside a ring. Sorting criteria were, for example, to sort numbers into more than 9, or exactly 13. If a number did not fit the criteria it could be jettisoned on a launch pad which made a humorous sound. The software will return a number to its starting position if the correct response is not given.

All of the children found the spoken instructions from the software difficult to understand, and responded by clicking at random on the objects on the screen, moving them at random at first into the circles or onto the launch pad. They worked out what to do by trial and error. The children decided for themselves who would operate the mouse. In each case, and without discussing this first, the mouse operator tended to say nothing, while the other child decided where the numbers should be put. This was particularly pronounced with two boys, as the one who did not control the mouse shouted: 'Put it there! (Pointing to the launch pad). Bin… bin… bin… It's not a six!' When the control of the mouse swapped to the other child, they also swapped their roles in terms of decision-making. Other pairs of children did not communicate between themselves at first, then the one who did not control the mouse began to give instructions (see Figure 3.1).

The children laughed at the screen reinforcement when the response was correct (the anthropomorphic elephant danced!) Even more amusing to the children was the launching of numbers which did not fit, as this was accompanied by some sound effects. One child became bored after trying one round of the activity. He persistently asked for a different game. His teacher commented that he had a very short attention span and was easily distracted.

Four of the children had access to a computer or Playstation at home. They all had good mouse control skills. None of them made use of the help button, which had been explained in the on-screen spoken introduction. If they made an error they tried again, often at random, until the number was correctly placed.

**Figure 3.1**   Year 1 pupils using Mighty Maths: Carnival Countdown

Each child was asked about the strategies that they might use if they were stuck. The responses included:

- Ask the teacher
- Think about the problem
- Count on my fingers
- Ask another child
- Push the space bar
- Use the delete key
- Cancel the game and try another one
- Try again
- Keep on trying again
- Use a calculator.

For Year 3, a quiz from Number Heroes was chosen. The six children were aged 8 to nearly 9 years of age. This software appealed to the children and in each of the observations of three pairs, the children chose to play against each other, rather than collaborate and play against the computer. Again, they were motivated by the multimedia effects. They took their turns with care, gave each other no help other than a grin if they thought that the answer was wrong, and enjoyed the opportunity to check each other's work.

At one point, David was stuck! He could not work out $16 \div \square = 2$. Then he murmured: 'Eight add eight is sixteen'. When asked how he had worked this out, he replied that he remembered this fact about sixteen. He was the only child who was seen to use a specific fact as a strategy to work out what he did not know.

All children were asked which strategies they might use if they were stuck. Responses were:

- Use cubes
- Look in my maths book
- Ask the teacher
- Ask another teacher (if Sir was busy)
- Ask a friend
- Get paper and pencil and work it out
- Use fingers
- Use a ruler as a number line
- Try again
- Make lots of guesses and choose the one that seems right.

*Comment*
In Year 1, apart from one child, the children really enjoyed the activity and wanted to continue with it when it was time for them to return to their classroom. They

enjoyed the multimedia effects, which compared well to the computer games which they had all played at home. They were motivated to continue even when they were getting wrong answers; however, none of them used strategies other than trial and error when they were unsure. Their list of strategies for when they were stuck did not relate to the computer activity. There seemed to be no connection for them between their class-based work and mathematics from the computer. Some of their responses were probably from their home experiences of computers: use the delete key; push the space bar; cancel the game and try another one.

Except in the one instance outlined above, none of the children made any attempt to use these strategies when stuck.

| | |
|---|---|
| Researcher: | Why don't you use your strategies when you work at the computer? |
| Rosie: | You use these when you're working in your books. We don't have things like paper and pencil or a ruler by the computer. |
| Researcher: | Why not? |
| Rosie: | Well ... I suppose you could, couldn't you! |

In Year 3 the children had begun to develop some strategies for dealing with difficulties. However, apart from one child, there was no evidence that they used any of these strategies when answering the quiz questions. Again, they did not make the connections between working at the computer and their class-based work.

The teachers, when questioned, commented that they believed that the children had a variety of strategies which they could use when they found a difficulty, and agreed that there seemed to be no connection for the children between class-based activity and the use of the computer.

## Case Study 2

At a primary school on the outskirts of a city, children in a Year 6 class were used to using Number Heroes. The ability range of the class was from level 2 to level 5. There was a bank of eight PCs set up in an area just off the classroom which was available for each class to use. Figure 3.2 shows the layout of this computer area in relation to the classroom. Teachers arranged to swap classrooms so that they could work with half their class using the workstations and the other half working in the adjoining classroom with them, then halfway through the lesson the children changed places with each other.

Children worked in ones or twos. During this one hour lesson about 16 children used the machines, with about half an hour at the computer. Two children set the machines up at the beginning of the lesson. The children working at the machines shut them down just before the end of the lesson, as requested by their teacher.

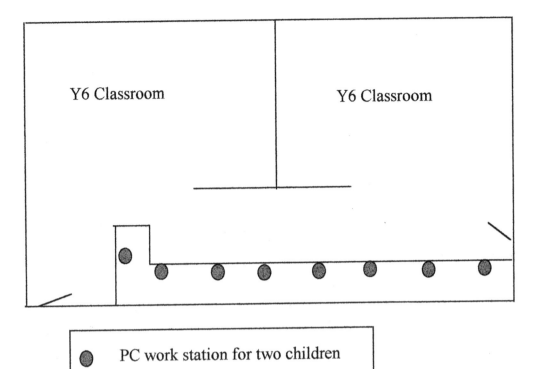

**Figure 3.2**   Layout of new computer area

The children had free choice within the Number Heroes options. Most of them preferred the quiz, and, unlike the other school, chose to collaborate rather than compete against the computer. They realised that the harder the questions the more points they won, and many children worked on very difficult questions in order to try to get a huge score (see Figure 3.3).

The following conversation occurred during observation of two of the children.

Researcher:   I don't understand how this works. What do you have to do?

Fred:   Erm, … they put this out … and you have to do the sum.

Researcher:   So you have to add up these two rows to make that answer and put in the missing numbers?

The children spent some time putting numbers into the sum. They didn't seem to be taking any account of place value and the size of their answer in any place. They pressed the 'done' button and were told that their answer was incorrect.

Researcher:   Before you change anything, how are you going to put it right?

Fred:   I shall have to try this one again.

Researcher:   Will you do it in the same way?

Fred:   Um … yeah, I'll try it again.

**Figure 3.3**   Year 6 pupil using Number Heroes

| | |
|---|---|
| Researcher: | Let's look at the question. What do you think that column has to add up to? |
| Fred: | (no reply) |
| Researcher: | Did you have to carry anything in your head from the first column? |
| Fred: | Yeah, I think I did, actually. |
| Researcher: | Supposing I hadn't been sitting here, what would you have done to answer the question? |
| Fred: | Try it again. |
| Researcher: | Suppose you got it wrong, twice, three times, four times ... what would happen? Would the program give you some help? |
| Fred: | No. |

Lilly, a very able girl, responded to questions about her errors.

| | |
|---|---|
| Researcher: | What do you do if it is not right? |
| Lilly: | Do it over and over again. |
| Researcher: | Do you have different ways of doing it? |
| Lilly : | No. |

The children were asked about the strategies that they used if they were unsure. They responded with:

• Use the calculator
• Ask Miss

- Ask each other
- Do it again.

One child had seated herself at the computer furthest away from her classroom. When observed, she grinned in a guilty manner. She had, against school rules, accessed the Internet, and was reading the Boyzone page!

The teacher, Rachel, discussed her children's progress during the year:

| | |
|---|---|
| Rachel: | They've used that program all year so whereas when they first started they were very unsure they will try at the highest level. They will challenge themselves. |
| Researcher: | They talked about the challenge. |
| Rachel: | Since we've been doing things like long multiplication and long division they'll have a go and challenge themselves. |
| Researcher: | They worked in pairs and talked to each other. |
| Rachel: | They're used to that. We encourage that so that they either play against each other or jointly against the computer. |
| Researcher: | Do you ever use any of the follow up activities in the handbook? |
| Rachel: | No. I think they get more out of actually what they're doing at the computer than if you turn it into a boring paper based task. At the moment the computer is very much a tool which you can use to get them to practise their maths without them necessarily realising it. |
| Researcher: | I wondered what would happen if they were stuck, if they found strategies,… trial and error… |
| Rachel: | They will have a go. If they do get it wrong then they don't see it as a big problem. I'm pleased with how they used that as there aren't any other maths resources. The fact that that has lasted all year shows that it is OK. |
| Researcher: | How often do you use the software? |
| Rachel: | With my class I would use it once a week. We set for maths. I don't use it much with the top set at all, just once a week for each child. They're much more capable of getting on with paper and pencil and practising. The lower ability use it much more often. |
| Researcher: | I noticed one child set herself a very average level, had success, and was very pleased with herself. |
| Rachel: | Yes. They [less able children] do tend to go for the easier levels, and to play safe. You can suggest that they go up a level, they know how to, and will do that. There are some who are quite happy to play the easier levels and others who really want to go to the top levels, even if it means coming and asking me how to do it! |

*Comment*

What was very obvious from the observations was how much the children enjoyed the challenge of the activities which they chose. The more able children tended to choose a level which was quite difficult for their ability. However, the less able carefully chose something within their capabilities and were pleased to be given a visual reward for each question that was correct. Again, there was little attempt by the children when working at the computer to use the strategies that they had been taught during their mathematics lessons. They did not seem to relate such strategies as doing a problem by a different method, using a combination of mental calculations and pencil and paper, as appropriate.

The one child who placed herself out of her teacher's sight and accessed the Internet (a serious crime at this school) does show how, when children are not observed, teachers cannot guarantee what activity is being undertaken.

## How the children responded to the software

In each case study the children seemed to really enjoy using the software. They were motivated by the multimedia approach, enjoyed the rewards from cartoon characters, and were eager to do well. Most of them were used to playing games on computers, had good control of the mouse, and were confident in using it. They seemed to enjoy the challenge, particularly in Year 6, and were motivated to stay on task until asked by their teacher to change places with other children.

## How they worked together

There was a clear difference in the first case study between the Year 1 and Year 3 children's approach. This may have been because the Year 3 children realised that the quiz would allow them to play against each other. However, the children in Year 6 chose to work collaboratively with the same software. This may be because they had used it over a much longer period of time than the younger children had, so that it was no longer novel to have an opponent. The Year 1 children, without any visible signs of communicating this, immediately undertook specific roles decided by whether or not they controlled the mouse.

## Strategies the children used when they gave the wrong answer or were stuck

The strategies used were in the main not those taught for mental calculation or for mental and pencil and paper methods. Rather, the children relied upon asking their teacher, or another child. They did not seem to relate the strategies that they had been taught in class-based work to working with the computer.

One or two children saw that apparatus could be used, such as cubes, the calculator or a ruler as a number line. However, none of them made any attempt to ask for these when stuck; instead they tended to rely upon random trials. A few children, particularly in Year 6, used trial and improvement methods, whilst being observed, but did not articulate this.

When asked the teachers were surprised that the children did not relate their classroom learning to computer work. It seems from this that teachers must make explicit to children that they can and must use these strategies when working with software. It is suggested that a specific list of possible strategies is drawn up, written down, and placed where children can access these, whether they are working at paper-based tasks or at the computer. Such a list might include:

- Use the mental strategies that you have learnt (with examples such as partitioning and recombining; totalling the tens first,…).
- Use a combination of mental and paper and pencil strategies.
- Use a number line or hundred square as an aid.
- Check calculations with an alternate strategy.
- Look back in your maths book for ideas on how to proceed.
- When working with a partner, discuss how you will proceed and try out different strategies.

This is not an exhaustive list. However, children do seem to need to be given permission to use these strategies in any situation.

## Teacher and child interaction

With a class to teach, there is very little time available for teachers to observe and interact with children working at the computer. This does mean that teachers have very little feedback about how children performed. Where there is a computerised record of success, this may well give scores, or percentages for correct responses. What it does not give is a breakdown of errors made, so that teachers do not have assessment evidence of success or misconceptions.

In order to make good use of such opportunities, children would benefit from discussion with an adult. This can be the teacher or a classroom assistant. This would give opportunities for children to be prompted to try another strategy, to explain their thinking, and, where they do not understand the question, for some teaching to be undertaken. It is also an opportunity for the adult to check that children are on task, for example not accessing the Internet, when they are supposed to be working at a mathematics activity, and are using their limited access to ICT profitably.

## Conclusions

Such software should not be used during the daily mathematics lesson because it is a solitary occupation, unlikely to be linked to the learning objectives of the lesson and the teacher will not have the time to supervise the activity. The Strategy does recognise that this type of program has its place and recommends that it is used at break or lunch-time, in after school clubs or as a homework activity.

Drill and practice software has improved since its introduction 20 years ago. Today's software should make good use of multimedia possibilities, particularly as it needs to compete in children's minds with the quality of the games that they play at home. It should (Ager 1998) be used to enhance provision, so the software used must be more exciting for the children than, for example, using workcards.

Effective use of the software depends upon children being actively encouraged to:

- use the range of mental calculation strategies taught through the numeracy lesson;
- use other strategies appropriately that they would normally use, such as paper and pencil, a number line, a hundred square, or, from Year 5, a calculator;
- discuss with their teacher or another adult, their thinking so that misconceptions can be identified and remediated;
- identify for themselves when they are having difficulty and to seek help.

## Integrated Learning Systems

During the early 1990s, evaluations of the use and effectiveness of ILS systems in primary and secondary schools were undertaken and reported by BECTa in 1998. The evidence for this section is taken from the BECTa findings, and from those whose research projects formed part of the report, as cited below.

BECTa (1998b) reported that ILS systems are not yet ready for unqualified endorsement. The potential to help pupils' learning is entirely dependent upon how it is used by schools.

### What is an ILS system?

The term Integrated Learning System (ILS) comes from the USA and is usually used to mean a computerised system which includes extensive coursework and a management system usually operating on a networked system. In mathematics it provides drill and practice to deliver the curriculum, through individualised tutoring and practice.

In order for teachers to manage the learning, an ILS system has three main components:

1. Curriculum content: this is an extensive tutorial, practice and assessment package, which covers a range of ability.
2. Pupil record system: this maintains the record for each pupil and records attainment.
3. Management system: this uses the individual records to produce a differentiated programme of work for each pupil.

(Underwood 1997)

An effective ILS system can make the initial assessment, then place the pupil onto an appropriate place within the system, thus taking account of prior learning. The management system will provide the teacher with up-to-date records for each pupil, and gives performance feedback to the pupil and the teacher. From the data that the management system collects it provides an individualised pathway through the curriculum, based upon its 'perception' of need.

The most common mathematics systems in use in primary schools are:

- **SuccessMaker** (Computer Curriculum Corporation, sold through Research Machines). This is a closed system, which produces a differentiated programme of work for individual pupils.
- **Global Learning Systems** is a more open system in that the teacher controls the material and the level at which the pupils work.

The key difference between these two systems is the degree to which control over individualised learning lies with the system, the teacher or the pupil (Underwood 1997).

## How it is used

In many primary schools that have adopted an ILS system for teaching mathematics, it is used for developing mathematical concepts with lower attainers. Pupils are expected to spend about 15 minutes each day, working at the computer on their own. The system will provide the task and some tutoring for new concepts. It will assess performance, keep a record of attainment, provide advice for the teacher on next steps in learning, and provide further practice where a pupil is finding new concepts difficult.

## The teacher's role

Within schools where the system operates effectively teachers had been trained in how to use the system effectively. Teachers need to understand (cited in Underwood 1997):

- The structure of the mathematics materials within the system.
- How to place pupils within the system.
- How to interpret system reports.

Research carried out on the impact of ILS systems in school (Underwood 1996) found five areas of impact on teachers who were involved fully in the implementation of ILS within their schools. These were:

- IT skills development: where teachers used the management system to provide updated reports on pupils' progress, and began to understand and use the wide range of the ILS resource, their own IT skills were improved, so that they were more positive in their use of IT and were willing to learn more about what the system could do for them. However, these improvements are not a major shift in technological skills for these teachers.

- Classroom practice: some teachers adapted their curriculum content to focus upon the needs of their pupils, as identified by the ILS reports. Others identified for themselves the parts of the curriculum tutored by the ILS which were weak, such as practical and investigative work. Others enhanced the range of experiences which their pupils received in the classroom, teaching skills which they may not have done for some time, because the system had acted as a reminder of the need for this. Some teachers found the depth of analysis contained within the ILS reports of great benefit, because these reports were far more detailed in diagnosis of need than they could produce themselves, with so many pupils in their class. For some, there was development of individualised work programmes for pupils.

- Learning styles: some pupils were encouraged to mark their own homework produced by the ILS system, so that everyone could compare how well they had done, at their own level. Some teachers encouraged their pupils to keep a record of difficulties that they met when using the system, which enabled the teacher to discuss with each pupil their progress, and for the reporting of difficulties to lie within the pupil's control. As the teacher responded to the concerns, it was seen that the relationship with the class and discipline improved, perhaps because the pupils felt that their teacher cared about their progress.

- Reflective practice: one teacher felt that the joy of teaching something new had been removed, because when trying to introduce a new topic to the class he knew that someone would have met it already on the ILS system. Another teacher noted that all benefited from the use of the system, that they were motivated by it in a non-threatening way, and wondered whether this was also so in her classroom interactions. She noted that the ILS corrected errors, without being offensive, and realised that one unfortunate comment from her would be far more damaging than anything that the ILS system 'said' to the pupils.

- Levels of collaboration: there was collaboration across ages between teachers in terms of pupil achievement and need, based upon the reports from the system. This has implications for pupils transferring from one class to another, or from one school to another, in that the ILS system can provide detailed records of attainment and need.

Other research from the USA (Clariana 1992) showed that teachers fell into five different categories of ILS users:

- **Novice non-participatory:** these teachers do not become involved, so that pupils receive the message 'this is not important'.
- **Novice:** these teachers lack the knowledge about the system and so cannot maximise the potential of using ILS. Over time, matters may improve, as teachers become more confident; however, attitude towards ILS will affect confidence.
- **Practitioner:** these teachers use ILS, especially for lower achievers, but teach the materials twice, once in class, and once through the use of ILS.
- **Integrator:** these teachers use ILS selectively, so that it matches more closely to classroom activity. All pupils do the same activities, so that the higher achievers are not extended.
- **Extender:** these teachers have fully integrated ILS into their classrooms so that work is covered through ILS, or in class, or through both.

These categories are indicative of teachers' levels of confidence and competence with using and managing ILS. However, Clariana (1992) also noted that as teachers move towards being extenders they teach pupils in small and smaller groups moving towards individual teaching programmes. This is not sustainable in England today, as the National Numeracy Strategy is quite explicit in its requirements of whole-class, interactive teaching.

## The effectiveness of ILS systems in primary schools

### Performance and pupil ability

Whilst the ILS system is supposed to provide each pupil with an individualised programme of work, appropriate to need, there is evidence that this may not always be the case (Underwood 1997). It may:

- Underestimate the starting level during initial assessment. This may be a deliberate policy on the part of ILS developers, so that the learning gains reported by the management system appear favourable.
- The system cannot identify the underlying knowledge base of the pupils' answers. This means that pupils may be provided with inappropriate material. They may have guessed an answer through lack of understanding or clicked on any answer because they were bored. The system then assumes misunderstanding, and gives new material to correct this.
- Pupils can become trapped at one level of the curriculum, because the tutoring system has not enabled them to learn. This is demotivating, and is likely to lead to repetition of activities at which they have already failed.

The more able pupil may be challenged, because if successful at a level, the system will introduce them to new, more challenging material.

## Attitude

Younger primary pupils had an improved attitude towards basic number work because the system was non-threatening in its way of working (Underwood 1997). However, the practical activities for mathematics, such as practical measuring, pattern making with shape tiles, must be provided by the classroom, as must the opportunity to interact with others, and discuss strategies used and solutions in solving problems.

## Self-esteem

Pupils' attitude towards mathematics is affected by their success. So often pupils have been taught that there is a 'right answer' required, through the use of closed questioning, and so pupils become anxious about giving an answer, in case it is wrong. With the ILS system pupils receive instant feedback on their performance, and without this being public to the rest of the class (Underwood 1997).

## Pupils' learning styles

In most schools, pupils were observed (Underwood 1997) working, on task, in an atmosphere of peace and quiet whilst engaged in an ILS session. This contrasted strongly with classroom work where pupils had more off-task interactions. However, particularly where pupils worked out of sight of their teacher, there was off-task behaviour, of, for example, remaining quiet but not engaging with the task, or of helping each other to manage the system.

## Attainment

It has been considered that ILS packages are of greatest benefit to low achievers; however, Underwood (1997) found that the pupils who made the most gains in mathematics were those who had a higher starting point. The most able sustained high levels of progress. However, they did not always feel that the concepts were presented in a manner which were helpful, and relevant to their age and maturity. There were insufficient questions available to enable the most able to demonstrate their understanding and problem-solving strategies. The ILS needs to take account of the range of problem-solving strategies which the more able will have, rather than expect the pupil to respond by using the ILS's chosen method. Many of the lower attainers achieved rates of progress on par with average pupils, who progressed relatively slowly when compared with the less and most able. Where there had been disruptive behaviour, this was reduced. Teachers noted that their pupils, through the repetitive practise of skills, had improved motivation, self-image and confidence. Some students who normally underachieved in the classroom, were better motivated by the structured practice offered by the ILS.

However, some pupils preferred the classroom interaction to the ILS, and underachieved when using the system.

For those pupils with Special Educational Needs (SEN) the system offers positive learning opportunities, particularly because it can break the learning down into small, manageable parts, which can be practised until understood. The ILS system gives much positive reinforcement, and pupils enjoy the on-screen rewards. However, the stress of the management system on providing a summary on performance can be counter-productive; it is not how many questions were right that is important, rather the recognition of the successful strategy in solving the problem (Lewis 1997).

For those pupils for whom English is a second language it was found (Underwood 1997) that they did improve their knowledge of mathematics, and it offered these pupils the opportunity to revisit work which they had found difficult. It helped to develop their concentration span, confidence, organisational skills, and independence in learning. But the gains must be offset by the negative points which were that the use of ILS disrupts other activities, it is very expensive to purchase, it is difficult to assess the true learning gains (rather than what the management system reports) and it reduces teacher control over the curriculum.

BECTa (1998b) noted that the use of ILS affected pupils; learning, and that the issue was 'not *if* pupils learn but *what* and *how* they learn'. Overall, BECTa noted that there was a 'significant and lasting effect for SuccessMaker on achievements in basic mathematical skills'.

*Management issues*
There was a difference in learning gains from school to school and that the reason for this was probably to do with the management and use of the technology in the classroom (BECTa 1998b). Schools which had positive gains in numeracy had managed to ensure that there was good quality of supervision for pupils using ILS and teacher intervention, to ensure that pupils' difficulties were dealt with promptly. However, the value of such an improvement should be assessed in the light of examination results: does the use of ILS for mathematics improve SAT results? (BECTa 1998b). Teachers need time to understand the management system, receive training in its use, and to become familiar with the curriculum content of the ILS package. This is costly and time consuming, and it can be questioned whether this is a cost-effective way of enhancing teachers' IT skills when compared to other possible ways (BECTa 1998b). They need time to observe their pupils working with the system. After the initial training, as teachers become more familiar with and confident in the use of the ILS, they will need further training so that its more advanced features can be used.

The use of an ILS system can be disruptive in terms of the timetable, so what pupils miss as they work at ILS must be taken into account. There may be geographical constraints as well, such as where the computers needed can be sited.

Even after two or three years, in some schools, it has been reported that teachers were still grappling with the problem of integrating it into the timetable, geography and curriculum of the school (BECTa 1998b). This is an expensive package for schools to purchase, and so it needs to be used to its fullest potential in order that schools have value for money from its use. Schools will need technical support, which again can be expensive; there is no point in having an ILS system if it cannot be used because of a hardware or software breakdown, and there is no technical support available (Underwood 1997). Schools need to consider the significant and enduring impact of ILS on the use of space and time within schools (BECTa 1998b), as computers will need to be networked in order to run from a server, and this will probably mean that a classroom or large space will need to be dedicated to computer use. Some head teachers reported (BECTa 1998b) that the impact of adopting an ILS system on parents, governors, and visitors to school, including HMI, had been positive.

Bagley (1996) argued that for pupils to benefit from using ILS, their work must be deemed to be important. If they are sent to work outside the classroom, or to the computer room, and their teacher does not carry out follow-up work with them based upon their ILS records of achievements, then the ILS work will not be seen to have any worth.

### ILS and mathematics pedagogy

If an ILS system is to help pupils to achieve high standards, then there are principles of construction of the system to consider. The issues are taken from BECTa (1998b) with additional questions and comments by the authors.

1.  Is there a match between the way in which problems and tasks are presented in class and in the ILS? If not, do pupils have the strategies to understand what is asked of them and to use their learning in order to solve the problems?
2.  What are the principles that identify the learning sequence? This question can be applied to any published mathematics scheme as well. Is there an assumption that particular skills must be taught and mastered before others?
3.  Is there more than one learning pathway? If all pupils follow the same learning pathway, on what evidence has this pathway been devised?
4.  Is it better to master basic skills first then to teach how these might be applied to problems, or better to start with problems and learn the strategies to solve them later? These are interesting questions, in that they take a different stance from the Askew *et al.* (1997) connectionist teacher, who believes that such learning, strategy and problem-solving, run hand in hand.
5.  With a new topic, is it best to start with concrete examples and move to generalisations, or to start with the general ideas and then move to specific

examples? The Numeracy Strategy builds from the concrete to generalisations, so a system that did not operate in this way would act quite differently from what is outlined in principle 1 above.

6. How does the system manage the learning process? When is feedback on performance given: during the task, breaking it down into its component parts, when perhaps an error has been made, or at the end?

7. Are the skills of solving problems transferable to other contexts? This is a particularly important question with regard to examinations, both SATS, and GCSE and beyond. Schools will wish to invest in a system only if there are measurable benefits of use.

8. In what circumstances do learners learn from their own errors, and when do these simply make learning more confusing and time consuming? Is learning from errors more likely to take place away from the computer environment, when it is possible to interact with others, to hear about strategies chosen and why, and to share solutions?

9. When a system notes an error how should it respond? Should it just point out the error? Give a hint? Provide a correct answer? Leave pupils to discover how to overcome the problem on their own? For many pupils, dealing with errors can be fraught; there is a sense of failure and perhaps loss of self-confidence and self-esteem when confronted with an error and not knowing how to deal with it. Systems should be supportive in their response.

10. How should the system respond if there is a period of inactivity? Is the pupil off-task? Thinking? How long before the system sends a 'reminder' to the pupil?

## ILS and the National Numeracy Strategy

It is quite clear from the National Numeracy Strategy (DfEE 1999) that ILS systems are not to be used as part of the Mathematics lesson. It states 'Individual use of computer programs is usually inappropriate in the daily lesson, except where pupils with profound special educational needs or exceptional ability are doing individualised work. But programs which allow pupils to practise number skills independently … have a valuable part to play in breaks and after-school clubs, and at home.' It goes on to say that 'repetitive practice of number bonds already mastered is not good use of lesson time.'

The place for an ILS system is then outside of the Mathematics lesson. This means that for schools which use a system other time must be found. The purpose of using the system needs to be questioned. Will there be value-added in terms of attainment for all pupils? Would those who are lower or slower attainers benefit? Will the more able be challenged? In view of the nature of the Mathematics lesson, its emphasis upon keeping the whole class together and aiming for high standards of achievement, teachers may decide to use such a system by identifying from their assessments the needs of particular pupils who are finding difficulty with particular concepts and skills and providing extra tutoring and practice through the use of the ILS system. This approach suggests that an open management system is needed, so that teachers can make informed decisions about their pupils' needs, as well as using the management data that the system provides about performance against particular mathematical topics.

However, the management of this learning is still problematic. Where is the system sited? How will the chosen pupils access it? Who will supervise them? The following case studies may help to answer these questions.

## Case Study 1

A large urban primary school set up a special needs base which included seven computers networked to provide Global mathematics. The school decided to offer mathematics booster classes, before the start of school in the morning, to try to improve the learning of those pupils who were likely to be borderline level 3/4 in their Year 6 SATs tests. Up to four adults worked with nine pupils and the pupils were encouraged to set their own targets.

The pupils felt special. They were doing this extra work in their own time, and really enjoyed the extra adult attention. They were able to focus their learning on their needs, consolidate their learning, and were able to set targets and see how they had performed against these. The SAT results of these pupils convinced the teachers that this way of working was worth continuing. The pupils all scored level 4, thus boosting their own self-confidence, and, of course, improving the school's SAT scores when compared against national averages.

Discussions with Jo, the coordinator for ICT, showed that the school intended to develop this further. Jo thought that future developments would include parents in the extra support sessions, learning alongside their children. This would have two effects: it would encourage the parents to take an interest in their children's learning, and would improve the standard of numeracy within the home. Another intention was to provide pupils with the opportunity of using ILS as a support for their Mathematics lesson learning, with time set aside for pupils to go to one of the computer rooms for focused individualised work.

## Case Study 2

The head teacher of a primary school on the outskirts of a small town had decided to set up a classroom as a computer centre, and to use SuccessMaker with the less able children. She would retire at the end of the school year, and saw this as something that she would begin, something that she believed in passionately, and something that she hoped that her staff would also begin to see as most advantageous for the children at the school. She persuaded her ICT coordinator (also the deputy head teacher) of the advantages of such a room, and the school successfully bid for National Grid for Learning support money. Together with a donation from the Parents Teachers Association the school had set up a dedicated ICT classroom, with 16 networked computers, a digital projector for whole-class or group teaching, and 8 separate computers, also networked, on which ran Research Machine's SuccessMaker. Ten staff had been trained in the use and management of SuccessMaker, including two Learning Support Assistants (LSAs), the ICT coordinator, and seven of the class teachers. The seven class teachers had been chosen because they were considered to be more willing to learn about the software and hardware, and to use it to the full advantage of the pupils in their classes. These teachers also were the younger members of staff, more recently trained as teachers, and more likely to have received some ICT input during their training.

The purchase of SuccessMaker for this school was to support the less able children. In each year group from Year 1 on, 16 children were identified as being likely to benefit from an intense programme of learning support. Their daily programme of work included withdrawal from their class for 40 minutes of support. Each group of 16 worked in two groups: 20 minutes in literacy, working with the two LSAs in the computer room, and 20 minutes working at SuccessMaker at both literacy and mathematics tasks. After 20 minutes the children swapped tasks. The two LSAs oversaw the children working at the computers, whilst also supporting literacy learning. The two LSAs were given some management time in order to review individual children's records on a regular basis.

The use of the computer room was timetabled so that it was in use all day, except for 40 minutes in the morning for assembly and playtime, and 50 minutes at lunch-time. However, the school had agreed that children could work with SuccessMaker before or after school, as long as a parent supervised them. After lunch there was a timetabled slot for the eight most able Year 6 children to use SuccessMaker for mathematics; these children would teach the next eight how to use it, and would be able then to access the computers before school, at breaks, or at lunch-times, as others took their place. Eventually the school hopes to set up homework clubs so that children can use the Internet to help them to research topics and to use SuccessMaker in order to improve literacy and numeracy skills. The school also intends to set up sessions for parents to learn or revise their ICT skills.

The seven class teachers who were trained were beginning to make use of SuccessMaker's management system to access their children's records so that they could make decisions about learning needs. Other staff were not computer-literate, and did not access the records, so that they were reliant on information being passed to them from the LSAs.

At the start of their 40-minute session the children entered the computer room eagerly, and were immediately seated at the computers. They put on headphones, logged on using their own password to the system, and began to respond to the questions. Each child could be seen to concentrate really hard on their work, there was no time-wasting and they appeared really motivated. They were not in competition with each other; instead they were interacting with the computer.

SuccessMaker asks a variety of questions for mathematics, so that children are challenged by the range of questions. However, it was noticeable that for calculation questions children's calculation strategies were mainly of the 'count on your fingers' type, and no adult observed this. The ICT coordinator believed that the management report would highlight how long it took to answer these questions, so that teachers would see that there was an issue. However, in order to understand what the issue is teachers need to see their pupils at work, and this is not possible as they are in the classroom with the rest of their pupils. The system also, of Year 3 children, asked addition and subtraction questions, of one- and two-digit numbers, in vertical form, which does not match with the National Numeracy Framework's requirement to delay the teaching of algorithms until at least Year 4. At the end of the mathematics session children saw their scores. The system works on an 80 per cent success rate in order to ensure that there is challenge. Children responded very positively to the gold stars, scrolls, or dancing bears, when they had a correct answer, and were eager to tell how many they had right in total at the end of the session.

Teachers reported how 'switched on' pupils were when they returned to class, and how much improved their mathematical performance was in the classroom. Teachers commented that children who attended these sessions had improved self-esteem and confidence. They were 'successful, independent, and joyful!'. The children who did not attend the sessions were able to work in smaller classes for 40 minutes each day, and this had benefited them, as they really enjoyed the opportunity to work with their teacher in much smaller groups.

## Conclusion

Both schools had made a large financial commitment to their IT facilities. Both schools were using ILS to improve the learning opportunities for their less able pupils, and both schools reported a good improvement in performance.

While there is no doubt that pupils are motivated by ILS, and by the opportunity to work independently, unless there is careful monitoring of achievement, and regular observation of pupils' strategies for solving calculations, teachers will not be aware of pupils' learning needs. It is not sufficient to check the management system records; how pupils respond to questions, the strategies that they adopt, and the efficiency and effectiveness of these must also be monitored, so that effective teaching for improvement in attainment can take place.

## Maths adventure and problem-solving software

### Background

Opportunities for pupils to 'use and apply' their mathematics skills and knowledge need to be created and although the strand heading has altered to 'Solving problems' in the National Numeracy Strategy, the emphasis has not diminished within government guidelines. Sub-headings such as 'making decisions', 'reasoning (and generalising) about numbers or shapes' and 'problems involving "real life", money and measures' now clearly indicate areas which pupils need the chance to explore.

The value of presenting contextualised mathematics problems for children to solve will be acknowledged, by primary practitioners, as an essential element of pupils' experience and development. While a child can perform calculations to obtain the correct answer to a sum, actually solving a worded problem may well cause difficulties. Extracting the essential facts, working out what operation and method needs to be used and then putting a numerical answer back into the context of the question being asked involves a variety of skills – pupils need the opportunities to develop and practise these. Transference of mathematical knowledge and skills to other apparently non-mathematical situations can also be problematic. This application of prior learning, across a range of situations, requires opportunities where this can be explored, experienced and developed.

In the early 1980s much of the software in primary schools was either drill and practice or adventure games. The quality, relevance to the curriculum and consequently the educational value of 'games' software was viewed with caution. While some programs were little more than 'arcade'-type games, others were considered to have a variety of beneficial effects. In addition to pupils finding the games fun and motivational, the software grasped and held their attention. For some children, this resulted in more sustained concentration and greater perseverance in order to complete the tasks presented. The interaction amongst pupils working at the computer was focused as they discussed the problems posed, made observations, decisions ... Children developed collaborative and cooperative skills.

With the introduction of the National Curriculum in the late 1980s, there was a shift in emphasis in primary schools from the use of game- and puzzle-type programs to word processors, databases, etc. Unfortunately, the place for the adventure and problem-solving software appeared to have disappeared, unless programs could be deemed as meeting the 'control and modelling' strand of the IT National Curriculum or have a strong subject content. However, Whitebread (1997) suggests that computer-based problems, particularly those set within the context of 'adventure games', are of value and offer a solution for teachers who find problem-solving activities difficult to organise and manage within the classroom.

### What do we mean by adventure games and problem-solving software?

Initially it is easy to assume that adventure games and problem-solving software are one and the same, as within an adventure game the user will have problems to solve. On closer inspection it becomes evident that this is not the case – there is a distinct difference between the approach and presentation of the two types of packages. Adventure games are usually characterised by an imaginary world into which the user is drawn and called upon to help solve a dilemma or quest. The fictional world carries pupils along so that they become engrossed in the story, relating to characters and events to solve the problem or reach the end of the mission successfully. Due to the nature of the software it tends to possess a more cross-curricular dimension, therefore the level of literacy required by the pupils has to be considered alongside the content of the problems to solve. Problem-solving software does not include the characters, events, story or mission. There may well be a scenario or context, which sets the scene for the problems, but these are not central to the program. The program focuses more directly on the problems to be solved.

### Adventure games and mathematics

Many pieces of dedicated mathematics software presently on the market are promoted as adventure games. However, these are, in essence, little more than 'drill and practice' exercises. The development of multimedia technology has led to the emergence of programs with, in some cases, high quality graphics, animation and sound. The entertainment value and initial 'seduction' factor can be very powerful; the question that teachers' must address is 'how can this software support and enhance the learning objectives identified?' or in other terms 'what educational role does this program serve?'.

As stated previously, adventure games are characterised by a fictional world with characters, events and a mission, quest or such like for the pupil to embark upon to reach an end goal. Along this journey the child encounters several problems to solve. While various adventure games may have some mathematical problems within them, these tasks may be in the minority when compared with the quest as a whole. Other curricula knowledge, skills and understanding may be required in order to successfully complete the challenge. Therefore, if such programs are to be used the teacher needs to consider:

(a) where in the curriculum they fit – it would be very difficult to justify the use of such software within the daily maths lesson;

(b) the maths concepts involved in the program – have the pupils encountered these? If not, there is little point in setting them off on a 'mission' they have no chance of completing.

Perhaps one of the best known adventures is Crystal Rainforest (Sherston); this does have cross-curricular links but the tasks are primarily designed to develop pupils' skills and understanding of Logo. Hence, in terms of mathematics, estimation of distance, angle of turn, identifying patterns and consequently building up of sequences are addressed. This would not be appropriate software to use within the confines of the daily mathematics lesson because it would not fit its format.

## Problem-solving and mathematics

There are numerous programs available which supposedly present problem-solving tasks but frequently are produced in such a way that the pupils need to input the 'right' answer; they lack openness and flexibility. However, many programs written in the 1980s are being reconsidered as their content relates well to the objectives in the NNS (reference is made to these at the beginning of this chapter, 'Useful little programs' or 'Legacy software').

The Micro-Smile series, published by the Microelectronics Education Programme (MEP), contain a variety of programs, which now may appear rather dated in terms of graphic quality, but in terms of concepts and content are sound. Each program is identified within the documentation by a category (e.g. place value, number patterns, logic, investigations) and these help to pinpoint which mathematical strands they primarily address. Many of these can be used to promote interactivity within the classroom, either in a whole-class or group situation. The teacher would need to spend time evaluating individual programs and selecting those that meet objectives set.

## Conclusion

It is more appropriate to use maths adventure games during break, lunch-times or after-school clubs than as part of the daily mathematics lesson. However, problem-solving software, which is open and flexible, may provide good opportunities for interactivity and so can be used during the mathematics session.

## Logo

Note: several different dialects of Logo exist, and it is entirely possible that the examples given below are in a different dialect from the one that is available to you. If so, please exercise some creative imagination.

One thing that sets Logo apart from all other computer applications in primary education is the sheer dedication and commitment of its enthusiasts. Since its original design over 30 years ago, many books and thousands of articles have been written about it. There is a Logo Foundation in the USA, and it has enthusiastic supporters in regions as diverse as Central and South America, Australia, Japan, the Middle East and Eastern Europe. It is also unique among ICT applications as it is mentioned by name in the English National Curriculum.

Logo is not strictly a computer program, but a programming language. It is the figurehead computer application of the constructivist approach to learning, which views knowledge as being created and constructed by learners themselves, in interaction with their environment. The chief creator of Logo, Seymour Papert, worked with constructivist psychologist Jean Piaget in Geneva before moving to the Massachusetts Institute of Technology in the mid-1960s to found the MIT Artificial Intelligence Laboratory. Logo was an offshoot of another programming language, Lisp, and it was developed over a number of years before it gained currency, first in American schools and then elsewhere.

Though it has many other functions, Logo is best known for its use of turtle graphics. There is nothing particularly cuddly about turtles, but they have their place alongside bears and fluffy bunnies in the anthropomorphic imagery of American childhood. The original floor-robot 'turtles' did not look particularly turtle-like, and, because of speed and memory limitations, early screen 'turtles' appeared as mere triangles. The turtle could move forwards or backwards, and rotate left or right. The intention was that children would be able to think of the movement as the turtle walking around the screen, leaving a trail to show where it had been. In more recent versions of Logo the screen turtle more closely resembles a turtle, and in many cases it can be reconfigured to look like whatever you like – a car, a bird, a helicopter, or a user-defined shape.

Papert's seminal book, *Mindstorms* (Papert 1980), sets out a whole philosophy of constructivist computer use. Computers were 'machines to think with', and the Logo language was a tool for learning.

You do not learn Logo for its own sake – you learn it in order to write programs to do something else. Logo is intended to be more or less immediately accessible to anyone, but to be capable of use at a very sophisticated level – to have a 'no threshold and no ceiling'. Originally, it was expected that, once they had mastered a few simple concepts and techniques, children would set themselves programming challenges, but in reality this has not always been this rosy, and it is often prudent to establish or negotiate tasks with children. Some very good Logo work can be done by children working alone, but it is often beneficial for children to work in pairs or threes, as powerful learning can take place as they formulate, test and modify their hypotheses about how to achieve their aims.

Simple programming is done by means of typing in a command, which is either a movement (FORWARD, BACK) or a turn (LEFT, RIGHT), followed by a number, which is either a distance to travel or an amount to turn (in degrees). Commands can be abbreviated (FD, BK, LT, RT). Turns are relative to the turtle's current orientation, and it is not uncommon to see Logo-using children inclining their heads and gesturing their hands round corners as they work out which way they want the turtle to go next. Sometimes reaching a solution is a matter of direct calculation, and sometimes it is a matter of estimation and calibration.

At no point does Logo suggest to users that they might be wrong. Because children are controlling the computer, rather than the other way round, Logo can make no assumptions about what users intend to happen, or what the 'right' answer may be. If the spelling or syntax of a command is entered inaccurately, Logo's response is 'I don't know how to...' or 'I don't know what to do with...'.

Users decide what they want the turtle to do, then devise a set of commands to make it do it. There is no expectation that they will 'get it right' first time, and certainly no noisy or bright reward for doing so. Users are thus encouraged to be adventurous and speculative, with no danger of being put down if they are not immediately successful. If the sequence does not produce the desired effect, users modify it and try again; this process can be repeated as many times as necessary.

Where Logo is used well, users soon learn that there are advantages in writing commands efficiently and elegantly. Thus, though it is possible to draw a square by entering FD 50 RT 90 FD 50 RT 90 FD 50 RT 90 FD 50 RT 90, it is far more efficient to use the built-in REPEAT function: REPEAT 4 [FD 50 RT 90].

Even greater efficiency and elegance can be achieved by defining procedures. Logo starts with a limited set of primitives (the things it knows how to do), and users can teach it new words, which encapsulate a series of commands. To define a procedure the user starts with the word TO, then adds a procedure name, then enters the series of commands, finishing with the word END. Thus the definition of a square might be:

TO SQ
REPEAT 4 [FD 50 RT 90]
END

Once it has been defined, simply entering SQ will make a square appear on the screen. It is often good practice to break down a task into separate units, particularly if these may be hierarchically organised, and if units need to be used several times. It also makes complex tasks more manageable if they can be defined in small units and then assembled into the whole. Thus:

```
TO PERSON
HEAD
BODY
LEFTARM
RIGHTARM
LEFTLEG
RIGHTLEG
END

TO HEAD
EYES
NOSE
MOUTH
EARS
HAIR
END
TO EARS
LEFTEAR
RIGHTEAR
END
```

…and so forth. Logo encourages the development of logical thinking, but it does not impose someone else's logic on children. More or less by definition, children come to their own understandings in a dynamic context – and often in a social context as well, through cooperative problem-solving.

Of course, it would be extremely dull if every square drawn had to be the same size as the one in our definition above, or if one had to write a new definition every time one wanted to draw a different-sized square. The solution, of course, is to introduce the concept of a variable. At this point, Logo begins to take on some of the characteristics of algebra, which is where many children have traditionally lost touch with mathematics (Thwaites and Jared 1997). In the context of Logo, however, the concept is not particularly threatening. Anyone who can define or nest procedures is already demonstrating a grasp of symbolic relationships. We can substitute a variable name for the value 50 in our SQ definition:

```
TO SQ :SIDE
REPEAT 4 [ FD :SIDE RT 90]
END
```

and then simply enter SQ 50, SQ 100, or whatever, to produce squares of whatever size we wish. Because the variable name is decided by the user, it can be obviously descriptive of its function (:SIDE), rather than obscure and quasi-mystical (*x, y*).

There are several ways in which early exposure to Logo should reap benefits in terms of mathematical concepts later. For example, children soon adapt to the idea that in order to turn the turtle through a right angle they need to use the number 90, to turn it by less than a right angle they need a smaller number, and so forth. This should pay dividends in terms of the understanding that angles measure rotation, and that the size of an angle between two lines is independent of the lines' length.

Left to their own devices, what do children do with Logo? Virtually everyone draws a square. When it comes to making a triangle, most users try REPEAT 3 [FD 50 RT 60], which does not work. Eventually, after some head-turning and gesturing-round-corners, or perhaps some heuristic, trial and error testing, they either come to an insight about exterior angles or else find the right solution without particularly knowing why it is right: REPEAT 3 [FD 50 RT 120].

Those who pursue the line of pattern-making might eventually derive a formula for making any polygon – something like:

```
TO POLY :SIDES
REPEAT :SIDES [FD 50 RT 360 / :SIDES]
END
```

followed by

```
TO ROLY :SIDES :TURN
REPEAT :TURN [POLY :SIDES RT 360 / :TURN]
END
```

If you are unfamiliar with Logo, try this for yourself. Enter the above definitions (carefully!), then type

```
ROLY 8 8
```

Clear the screen with CS, then enter ROLY again, with two more values. For many years children have been delighted with the glorious spirograph effects that can be created, see Figure 3.4. Examine the two definitions, and decide how they work. Perhaps substitute a third variable (say, :LENGTH) for the 50 in POLY, then edit ROLY so that there are three variables in it (i.e. TO ROLY :LENGTH :SIDES :TURN, etc.).

It does not follow that what children will naturally wish to do is create pretty geometric patterns. Many would rather draw houses, dogs or cars, and their definitions may be very long-winded and haphazard. There is much to be said for defining parts of a drawing as procedures, as it saves an enormous amount of retyping every time the sequence is re-run.

The progression from simple commands to sequences of commands, to repeat loops, to procedures, to variables does not happen overnight of course, and neither do children discover the vocabulary and syntax of the next stage for themselves. Teachers need to observe and monitor children's Logo activities sensitively, and judge when it is best to give children the space to think things through for themselves without adult intervention (this can be a very powerful learning process), and when a well-chosen question or hint might help to scaffold the activity and reduce frustration. The important point is not to take the ownership

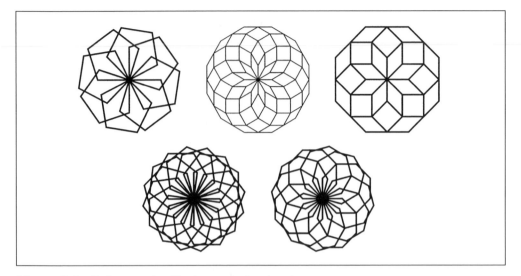

**Figure 3.4**  Spirograph effect, created using Logo

of the task away from the child through heavy-handed intervention or by trying to make children reach conclusions for which they are not ready. A new idea, like, say, the concept of the procedure, is best introduced at the point where knowing how to do it will permit the individual or group to solve a problem which might otherwise flummox them. Of course in practice things do not always work out as neatly as that, and there is a case to be made for some direct teaching of Logo techniques to a large group or even a whole class (Ainley and Goldstein 1988, Blythe 1990). This should never be presented in a vacuum as direct instruction.

Analyse the following example of how not to do it, and decide how it could have been done better. (If you do this in a lecture, staff meeting or in-service course, you might like to role-play it, and then discuss issues that arise.)

## Mr Hogg teaches Logo

Mr Hogg is the ICT coordinator. He has been a computer enthusiast for years, and knows a lot about hardware and software. His class are in the computer room, sitting two-to-a-machine (see Figure 3.5). They don't say much.

"Right, class – today you're going to learn how to draw a square using a repeat loop.

Are you ready? Has everybody got Logo running on their machine? Good.

How many sides does a square have? Yes, four – well done. So our loop is going to repeat four times.

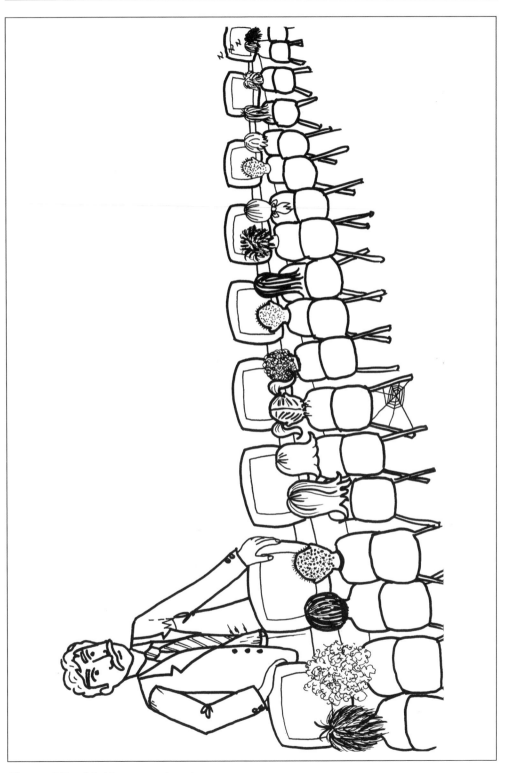

**Figure 3.5** Mr Hogg teaches Logo

Type in REPEAT – R..E..P..E..A..T.. – don't spell it wrong or it won't work – then leave a space and type the number 4. Don't forget the space, or it won't work.

Now put in a square bracket. It's next to the letter P on your keyboard. Don't use a round bracket or it won't work.

Now type in FD for forward.

All done that? Now we need to decide how long to make the side. I think we'll make it 50. Type in 50.

Yes, you do have to leave a space between the FD and the 50. I didn't say that because I assumed you already knew. You always have to leave a space after FD. We did that last week.

Leave a space after the 50 and type in RT because we need to make the turtle turn right.

What was that, Richard? Why not left? Because we're turning right, that's why.

How far have we got to turn? Yes, it's a right angle, because squares have right angles. And what's a right angle? 90, that's right. Type in 90. Yes, you do have to...

Now close the square bracket. It's next to the other one.

OK, you've written your repeat loop – don't do anything else until you're told to.

Laura, read out to me exactly what you've typed in. Good, well done.

Everyone else, have a look at the screen next to you and see if you think they've got it right.

OK, when everybody's ready, press Return, and what have you got? A square! That's right.

No, Simon? Well try typing it in again, and this time leave spaces between things. Well done.

Now you know how to write a repeat loop. Next week I'll teach you how to use variables.

Now see if you can make another square with sides of 60..."

Most primary teachers are constructivists at heart. They know very well that learning does not proceed in a linear fashion, and that what is absorbed and retained from any shared learning experience is different for each child and not entirely predictable. At first sight the philosophy that underpins Logo seems to be at odds with the view of education that permeates the National Curriculum (and in particular its assessment), and also at odds with prescriptive structures like the

National Numeracy Strategy. Paradoxically, the architects of both have expressed approval for Logo, and have recognised its power and value.

One way to teach Logo is as a dialogue with the class or group, with the teacher taking on the role of the ignorant and innocent assistant who merely puts into effect the wishes of the children, but who occasionally asks pertinent questions: 'What do you want me to do? Why do you want me to do that? Does it have to be done that way?'

Alternatively, it is possible to set up whole-class activities in, say, estimating and calibrating which rely on Logo as the medium of delivery. A simple example might be to present a screen with a fixed point in the middle ('home'), and a number of small islands, labelled A, B, C... at various intervals around the periphery. This could be accomplished either by using a version of Logo that permits background graphics, or else by fastening an acetate sheet to the monitor. Children are asked to define as a procedure the turtle's route to island A in just two commands, one a turn and the other a distance. Initially they are asked to guess how far the turtle would need to turn and how far it would need to travel. Both commands are entered (preceded in this case by a HOME command), and then repeatedly modified until the turtle arrives exactly at its intended destination. This is then recorded as a procedure:

TO A
LT 23 FD 88
END

Children are then invited to estimate the turn and distance to island B (either from home or else from island A, depending on the story that is woven around the activity), and so forth. Within a short while, most children can estimate turn and distance with considerable precision. Of course, one could argue that this is not in itself a useful skill, as the distances apply only in the context of the specific screen and specific exercise, but this would be a mistake. Being able to reason: 'Well, the distance to A was 88, and the distance to B was 123, and C is somewhere between the two, so I'd say it was about ...105' is a fairly fundamental, useful and transferable skill.

Some recent versions of Logo have sought to harness the *modus operandi* of modern machines by making extra facilities available that would not have been possible 30 years ago. This is sensible when one is dealing with structural features like loading, saving and printing, but is probably better avoided when it changes the way children interact with the programming language. In some versions, for example, it is possible to click anywhere on the screen and make the turtle move automatically to that point. Having such a facility turns Logo into something else, and substantially diminishes the computer's power as a 'machine to think with'. This tendency is an insidious subset of the Technological Imperative, which should be resisted. Many Logo enthusiasts retain their commitment to 'classic' Logo:

'What do we mean by "classic" Logo? We mean a traditional Logo:

- that matches the environment described in Seymour Papert's *Mindstorms*, which woke countless educators to the power of Logo learning;
- that has no threshold and no ceiling;
- in which the user moves and turns a turtle using forward, back, right, and left commands;
- in which the user can add new words to Logo's vocabulary by defining new procedures using the TO command;
- in which the user can look at all the procedures that make up his or her program;
- that is compatible with the Logo examples and activities found in many maths texts and resources;
- that is suited to all levels and all abilities;
- in which everything that can be done with "point and click" can also be done using a command;
- that is a complete programming language, useful to even the most accomplished programmer.'

Incidentally, it is worth bearing in mind that when Logo was first introduced, most children had no other way of drawing on the screen. It is probably not possible to gauge whether exposure to high-resolution graphics and painting software has had any effect on what children choose to draw when using Logo.

## Floor turtles

Today's floor turtles are usually free from computer control, in that they have their own, inbuilt, computer. These are programmable from buttons set into the machine. There are two types normally met in school:

- Roamer, made by Valiant Technology Ltd, which can have its basic settings for length and angle changed, so that the size of the number input is accessible and understandable by pupils of a particular age and stage. The standard settings enable Roamer to turn in degrees, so that an input of 90 would result in a turn of 90°, and a distance input of 1 would result in Roamer moving 30 cm, because the basic unit of movement is one Roamer length (Roamer's diameter is 30 cm).
- PIP, made by Swallow Systems, which has an option for multiplying all variables by ten, in order to make the number size accessible to young children. For example, with the use of the 'times ten plug' angles become multiples of ten, so that for 90° an input of 9 is sufficient. The standard settings, without the 'plug' fitted, enable PIP to move 1 cm for a distance input of 1, and to turn 90° for an input of 90.

Both of these systems also have keys which are programmed for left or right turns, and for forward and backward movements. Both systems also have the opportunity to write procedures, which the turtle 'remembers' until it is switched off, and can be programmed to play a tune.

These systems have been used as a precursor to using screen based Logo in many primary schools. However, for many pupils there is little transference between using Roamer or PIP on the floor, and using screen based Logo, set in the vertical plane. It may be that with Roamer or PIP, the opportunities to physically walk the planned route help pupils to understand the movements that Roamer and PIP need to make, while with screen based Logo, fingers can move across the screen, but the angle of turn is an issue. Both systems have cumulative memories, that is whatever was programmed becomes the first part of the next set of movements, unless specifically erased.

Roamer can be 'dressed', by decorating specially made covers as, for example, pirates, a dog, a fancy hat. PIP can 'wear' a costume designed to turn it into an animal. For young children this anthropomorphism can encourage them to believe that, for example PIP, is a real creature.

Traditional use of Roamer and PIP includes:

- Estimation of size of angle and direction of turn: for example, estimating how far Roamer needs to turn in order to be able to turn the corner in a maze.
- Estimation of distance: estimating how far Roamer must move in order to reach the cupboard.
- Addition and subtraction: combining movements that have been tried to move a given distance in one movement; for example 'Roamer moved forward 2, then 6; that was too much so I moved it back 1. I shall now try 7 (2 + 6 – 1)'. The addition and subtraction is a by-product of estimation of angle and distance, rather than the purpose of the activity.
- Understanding negative numbers: moving Roamer along a floor based number line, forwards and backwards, in order to explore what happens when moving from positive to negative numbers. This can be time consuming, and the same results can be achieved more easily by asking pupils to jump along a floor based number track, or by using desk number lines (see Figure 3.6).

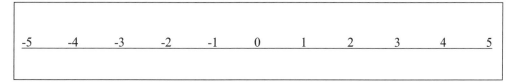

**Figure 3.6**   A number line for Roamer

- Understanding variables: programming Roamer to repeat a given movement, changing one of its components. Repeat 4 times (Forward 2, right 90) will produce movement which describes a square. Change Forward 2 to Forward 3, and the square grows in size. Change Repeat 4 to Repeat 6, and Roamer will describe the square and repeat the first part of it. Change right 90 to left 90 and Roamer will describe the square in anticlockwise fashion.

## Using Roamer or PIP in the classroom

*Power.* Both systems are powered by batteries. PIP has a rechargeable battery built in which needs recharging regularly. Roamer can either run on rechargeable batteries or on lantern batteries. When the batteries are running down, in all cases, the turtle's movements become inaccurate and erratic. Roamer has been known to move in circles, whatever the input! It is important before the teaching session begins to ensure that the turtle has full battery power. If the batteries run down any procedures placed in the memory will be lost, as these cannot be stored permanently.

*Teaching.* Roamer and PIP can both be used as part of teacher demonstration. For example, with children and teacher sitting in a large circle, the teacher might demonstrate how to program Roamer so that it moves from teacher to a child sitting opposite and back again. Individuals might then be challenged to input a Forward command to send Roamer to the child sitting opposite. This can become more complicated with the addition of a Right or Left command and a Forward one to reach pupils sitting at other parts of the circle. Group work could then include pupils working together to program Roamer to move from one part of the classroom to another.

## A classroom scenario

Three children are working with Roamer on the carpet area. Their task is to use estimation skills for distance and angle in order to move Roamer around a given pathway. Roamer is decorated as a postman, and carries some letters on 'his' back. On the carpet are some large cardboard boxes, decorated as house fronts. Roamer must visit each house, and the children will put the relevant letter from Roamer's back into the house. They begin by estimating how much they need to make Roamer turn in order to be in line for a straight movement to the first house. One of the children acts as scribe, writing down their commands using Logo-type language. Using the first letter of the command words (F: forward; B: back; R: right; L: left) he writes: R 30 F 6. The children carry out this command and find that Roamer has disappeared off the edge of the carpet. They discuss what is wrong, and decide that Roamer should have turned to the left, not right. So they cancel that command, and this time try L 30 F 6 and find that Roamer this time goes in a straight line to the house, and overshoots it. They return Roamer to the starting point, and try again: L 30 F 4 and Roamer arrives at the house. They continue in this way until all the letters have been delivered. Their teacher wants them to demonstrate their Roamer letter delivery to the other children so they then program in the corrected movements, and towards the end of the lesson show their results.

*Written records of commands*

Pupils must keep a written record of commands. They are unlikely to remember the commands that they programmed into Roamer, and so will be unable to refine their estimations. By keeping a list of commands, they can also see where it is appropriate to use the Repeat command. They can also use their list to help them to program a series of movements as a procedure.

## Conclusion

The philosophy upon which Logo is built encourages problem-solving and investigative work in an interactive environment which fits well with the demands of the National Numeracy Strategy. It can be used as an aid during the main teaching activity where the whole class can participate in discussion, as well as during grouped and paired work.

## Data handling software

### Background

'Handling data is the most obvious area in which pupils can use IT to support their work in mathematics.' (BECTa 1998a)

Data handling as a theme overlaps considerably in terms of mathematics and ICT; therefore in satisfying the requirements for handling data in the National Numeracy Strategy, many aspects of the National Curriculum for ICT will also be addressed. However, use of data handling software does not automatically mean that pupils are addressing or developing mathematical concepts and skills. Activities need to be planned whereby appropriate software is selected to meet specified learning objectives. Therefore, as with all programs, it is essential that the teacher has the time to explore the facilities and features of specific packages to ensure that the ICT is suitable and helps to meet the aims of the lesson.

In addition to the close relationship between mathematics and ICT, data handling does have a truly cross-curricula nature. The focus of a data collection may well be, for example, scientific or geographical, hence the skills and concepts required to carry out an investigation successfully will also involve the application of mathematical knowledge, skills and understanding.

## What is data handling?

Data handling involves the collection, representation and interpretation of data or information. *Data* and *information* are often used to mean the same thing although strictly there is a distinct difference between them. *Data* is the raw material collected, whilst *information* is the format whereby the data has greater structure or makes more sense. For example, Figure 3.7 shows data and Figure 3.8 shows information.

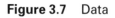

|     |     |      |     |
| --- | --- | ---- | --- |
| **F** | **Amy** | **1992** | **2** |

**Figure 3.7**  Data

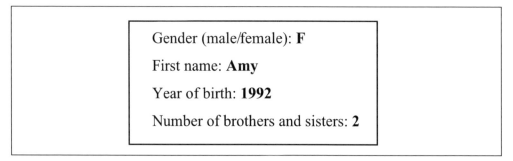

Gender (male/female): **F**

First name: **Amy**

Year of birth: **1992**

Number of brothers and sisters: **2**

**Figure 3.8**  Information

The collection and representation stages of the data handling process usually pose few problems in the primary school as both a purpose for and the focus of a relevant data handling activity can be easily identified. The data is 'used' by the asking of simple questions which require children to 'read' a graph or table. Questions where pupils have to think, interpret, reason and offer ideas are not pursued as frequently. Unfortunately, with a lack of emphasis on developing pupils' higher-order information skills the interpretation aspects are quite often neglected.

## The impact of data handling software

The introduction of data handling packages in school made it possible to display data easily in a variety of forms. At a click of the mouse, the format could be changed from a block graph to a pie chart, line graph or scattergram. Consequently, comparison and analysis of different forms of display of the same data could easily be undertaken. Discussions concerning the most appropriate format for a particular set of data, the ease of 'reading' each display and specific features of certain graph types could also be explored. Creating graphs using ICT also meant that more time could be spent on extracting and interpreting information as pupils did not have to hand-draw the graphs first. However, evidence suggests that the software was largely used to produce impressive graphical displays of data collected and little time was then spent on using them to interpret their contents (NCET 1994). Dedicated graph-plotting software or database packages can be used to create graphs. These will be discussed at greater length in the forthcoming pages.

Access to computer-held databases also opened up new avenues in terms of information handling. The speed at which the computer could sort and search data meant that the process was much faster than that done manually and hence in addition to being able to carry out investigations more quickly, much larger stores of data could be used. Creation of a data file is, on the whole, the responsibility of the teacher, although at upper Key Stage 2 it is suggested that children create a simple file (National Numeracy Strategy). Whilst software aimed at Key Stage 1 is usually easy and simple to use, both in terms of interrogation of an existing file, and also the creation of a file structure, this is not always true of packages deemed suited to Key Stage 2. The setting up of a new file can appear quite daunting when software is unfamiliar and you have little or no previous experience of creating a database from scratch. If the purpose for collecting information is clear with questions you wish to ask or hypotheses to be tested stated, then the task of creating the file is somewhat easier. Due to time constraints and lack of knowledge and skills with software, creation of data files by teachers for pupils to input data and then use, has been addressed less effectively than use of pre-existing files.

Spreadsheets are another type of generic software that handles data. However, their impact, in our experience, has been very limited in the primary classroom; personally, we feel the reasons for this are two-fold. Firstly, many teachers have never had to use a spreadsheet and the word conjures up images of rows upon rows of figures that are used to carry out complicated or mysterious calculations. For many, this can appear like a nightmare! Secondly, for a primary practitioner, the idea of using a spreadsheet may seem totally irrelevant or of negligible value to the learning of their pupils. Over the past few years, we have noted with interest and some degree of alarm, the frequency with which spreadsheets are referred to and used in exemplars for primary use. Much of this appears to be 'watered' down higher-level mathematics work, which is not necessarily appropriate to the needs of primary-aged pupils. However, there are certain situations where a spreadsheet could be used. These will be discussed in the review of spreadsheet software.

A review of a selection of graph-plotting programs, databases and spreadsheets follows. The miscellaneous section considers various pieces of software currently available which claim to address aspects of data handling.

## Graph-plotting software

Graph-plotting software is that dedicated to producing graphical representations of the data that the user inputs. Simple to use, packages exist for pupils in both Key Stages 1 and 2. The range of presentational formats and features vary dependent upon the program.

**Pictogram** (CECC, Acorn) – appropriate for use in Key Stage 1, this software contains a selection of topics (age, colour, eyes, hair, houses, months and weather) from which a choice is made. Once a topic has been selected, a set of related pictures (or icons) appear at the bottom of the screen (e.g. Journey – lollipop person and children to represent walking, a double-decker bus, a coach, a bicycle, a car and a taxi). By selecting and dragging the chosen modes of travel and numbers of each to the graph window, a pictogram develops. At any point if the wrong icon is selected it can be returned to the bank at the bottom of the screen, by the 'select and drag' method. As the pictogram is created the horizontal axis is numbered 1, 2, 3... to indicate columns, however the user can enter text labels. The vertical axis remains blank – one picture representing one item, as shown in Figure 3.9.

In addition to pictograms, the data can be displayed as a block graph or bar chart, these icon options are located at the bottom left of the screen and selection via the mouse enables the user to view these formats. A graph 16 columns wide and 40 pictures high is the maximum permissible size; however at this size it cannot be viewed in totality on screen and the scroll bars have to be used.

The menu (accessed by clicking the middle mouse button) toggles between the main options and the pictures of the topic selected. Within the main options are the facilities for printing, saving, creating a new display or selecting a new topic.

Care is needed when using this software to ensure that the children place the appropriate icon in a column, as any icon can be placed in any column. This is an important discussion point and will help children to realise that each column should display like information.

**Graph Plot** (SEMERC, Acorn and PC) – suitable for Key Stages 1 and 2, this will produce simple bar, line and line bar graphs and pie charts. As you run the software two windows appear, side by side. The left-hand window is where you enter your data and as you do so the graph is created, entry by entry, in the window on the right. The software automatically determines and adjusts the scale of the axes and a key is developed. The user enters a title for the graph and can also alter the headings for the two columns headed 'Name' and 'Number' in the data entry window. It is important to be aware that if data connected with colours is the focus then the bar graph or pie chart produced can be rather confusing, especially

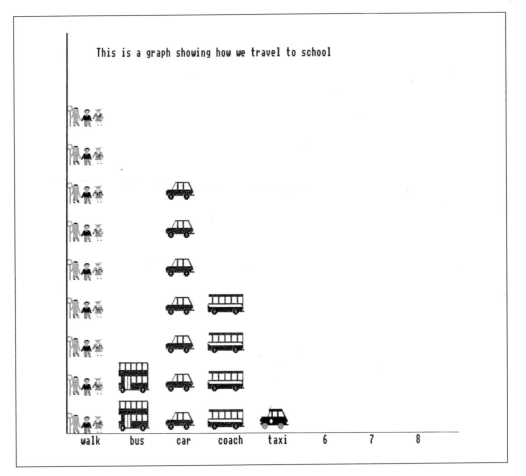

This is a graph showing how we travel to school

walk    bus    car    coach    taxi    6    7    8

**Figure 3.9** 'Journeys' pictogram, created in Pictogram

for younger pupils. The computer has a predetermined order for the colours of the display – if favourite colours is the focus then the actual colour of the columns does not necessarily match up with the data. However, this can certainly be used as a discussion point considering how computer generated displays compare with hand-drawn, or how a piece of software does not have the 'intelligence' to match the data entry and the subsequent display.

The menu (middle mouse button for Acorn) provides the options to select the graph format, print, save or alter the display.

*Printing and saving*
The option to print the graph is a standard feature within graph-plotting software. This provides a hard copy of the data display and further work away from the computer screen, related to extracting and interpreting information, can also occur. Both impact, and on occasions clarity, can be lost somewhat if the printout

is in black and white. It is also worth checking whether the key is printed with the graph as without this the columns, lines, points or sections of the display have little meaning. Graph Plot has an option to print the graph in 'outline' rather than colour. This can be a useful alternative, particularly if you do not have access to a colour printer, or if the focus of the data display is colour related; pupils can then fill in the key and columns or sections by hand in the correct colour, as shown in Figure 3.10.

Graphs can also be saved for use at a later date or exported into another application such as a word processor, where they can form part of a report, for example, of a science investigation.

*Considerations when selecting graph-plotting software*
The teacher needs to spend time evaluating the program prior to its use within a lesson to establish if it offers what is required and to explore the facilities and features to ensure that they are adequate and appropriate. Consider:

- What graphical formats are available – e.g. pictogram, bar chart, line graph, pie chart, scatter graph.
- Can the orientation be selected? (Horizontal or the more standard vertical.)
- Does the software calibrate and determine the scale?

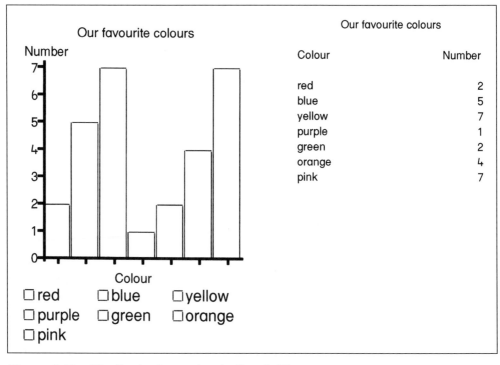

**Figure 3.10**   'Outline' print option in Graph Plot

- Can the scale, on the created graph, be switched on and off?
- Is the key displayed on screen?
- Are the axes labelled appropriately?

*How can graph-plotting software be of value to mathematics?*
Due to its ease of use and speed of data display, this software provides a means by which various graphical formats of the same data can be compared – questions such as 'Is the presentation fit for its purpose?' can be addressed. A pie chart may not present data in the most appropriate format and specific information may be more difficult to extract. Similarly, issues related to the use of line and scatter graphs, which are suited to certain types of data, can be explored.

Hand-drawn and computer generated graphs can be compared to establish their similarities and differences and consider why, for example, two bar charts presenting the same data may look quite different. They may have different labels or scales for their axes.

Whilst pupils do need to have experience of constructing a variety of types of graphs, they do not need to hand-draw them on every occasion. The focus may well be on extracting information and interpreting the data – the data handling process does not end after collection and representation. Opportunities for pupils to develop higher-order information handling skills need to be provided.

## Databases

Database software stores information. Each separate collection of data is known as a *file* and each file contains *records* and within each record there are *fields*. For example, you may set up a data file about the pupils in your class, each record would contain the information about one child and the fields would be the questions asked or the areas of data collected, such as surname, first name, date of birth. Field types vary dependent upon the type of data to be gathered – names entail text, ages may require an alphanumerical field, whilst number of siblings would be numeric. The thinking, design stages and construction of a file are essential for it to be of any value. The purpose of a data file must be clear, the areas for data collection decided and hence the fields and their types determined prior to its creation.

The range of features for creating a file varies from program to program. **FindIt** (Appian Way, Acorn), which is appropriate for use with Key Stage 1, provides a structured framework via questions or options when creating a file, the first of which is for the number of fields (1–20). Next the user selects from three field types (word, number or date) for each field. The basic file structure is then created as the field names are entered. Additionally, an extremely useful 'key word' facility means that the most likely responses can be entered and therefore when data is input these key words can be displayed on screen to choose from. If, for example, data is collected about pets, the common animals can be listed (e.g. dog, cat, rabbit, hamster, guinea pig) and then the problem of children inputting a variety of spellings for one animal can be overcome. Other advantages of this feature include:

- time is saved as pupils input their data as they just have to click on the appropriate response;
- when the file is interrogated, search results will yield accurate information (if a response is spelt in four different ways, a search will only show the records corresponding to the spelling used for the search).

However, this does also highlight the value of thinking through the possible field responses and the preliminary work done with pupils prior to creating the file structure. Always consider responses such as 'none' or 'other' as a 'catch-all' strategy.

Other database software (e.g. **Junior Pinpoint** (Logotron, Acorn and PC)), more suitable for Key Stage 2, has a greater flexibility and range of facilities. For example, for field types the choice includes text, numeric, yes/no, multiple choice and date. Within the numeric option you can limit the values, allow negatives, have units specified, as shown in Figure 3.11.

The presentational features within Junior Pinpoint provides the facilities to create a professional looking survey or questionnaire and there is the option of including graphics as well. This can be printed for pupils to complete as they collect their data prior to input into the computer.

After the file structure has been created the data can be entered and then questions asked. Although the National Numeracy Strategy does not specify the use of a computer database within the objectives or examples for Key Stage 1 this does not mean that the teacher cannot make use of an existing file for pupils to ask questions of, sort and search. At Key Stage 2 however the National Numeracy Strategy suggests not only using an existing file but also making a simple computer database (Year 6). Sorting a computer-based file can be compared and contrasted with a paper-based version, for example with a class data file, placing all records in alphabetical order by surname. Searching facilities can be used to answer questions or test hypotheses.

Database software also enables the creation of graphs, either using all the records in a file or just those identified as a result of a search. However, it is important to view carefully those produced based on the results of a search as it is possible to create graphs that have little or no value and at times do not make sense.

Functions to calculate basic statistics, such as range or mean average, are also available within some programs.

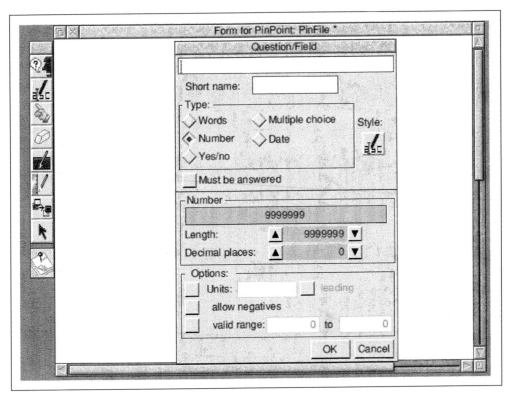

**Figure 3.11**   Field types within question menu of Junior PinPoint

## Spreadsheets

Spreadsheets enable the presentation of data in a tabular, row and column format. Although spreadsheets have been increasingly referred to in government documents, experience suggests that primary practitioners do not consider their use appropriate or applicable for their pupils, particularly at Key Stage 1 and lower Key Stage 2. Part of this view may be linked to teachers' lack of personal knowledge and use of spreadsheets or until more recently the existence of very few user-friendly spreadsheets produced for the educational arena. Figure 3.12 shows a typical spreadsheet format.

The idea of a spreadsheet used as a tool/resource by the teacher to aid in, for example, the exploration of number patterns, sounds reasonable. However, some means of all the pupils seeing the screen image is imperative. If the teacher has a large monitor, a data projector or interactive whiteboard, then this enables whole-class teaching – the standard computer monitor with 30 children is not viable.

Various approaches can be taken where pupils are using the software:

- exploration of an existing file to answer questions, carry out calculations, hypothesise and make predictions;
- as a tool to assist in the investigation of a numerical problem;

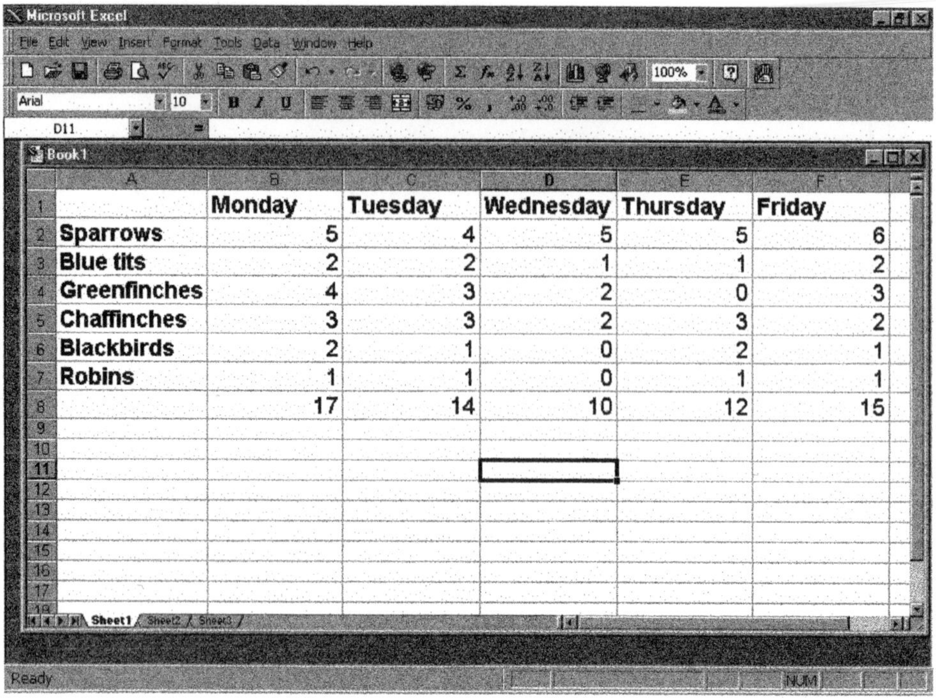

| | Monday | Tuesday | Wednesday | Thursday | Friday |
|---|---|---|---|---|---|
| Sparrows | 5 | 4 | 5 | 5 | 6 |
| Blue tits | 2 | 2 | 1 | 1 | 2 |
| Greenfinches | 4 | 3 | 2 | 0 | 3 |
| Chaffinches | 3 | 3 | 2 | 3 | 2 |
| Blackbirds | 2 | 1 | 0 | 2 | 1 |
| Robins | 1 | 1 | 0 | 1 | 1 |
| | 17 | 14 | 10 | 12 | 15 |

**Figure 3.12** Spreadsheet format, Excel

- creation of a spreadsheet based on real data and for a specific purpose, e.g. a school shop – record of stock, items, quantity, purchase cost per item, selling cost per item. This can then be used to calculate profits, by adjusting selling costs the pupils could see the effects on profits, etc.

Alternative software to standard spreadsheet format is now available. One such package is **Maths Frames** (NW SEMERC, Acorn and PC), which the publishers consider to be 'a truly graphic spreadsheet'. This is geared towards Key Stage 1 and comes with five pre-set scenarios (garden, money, shopping, traffic and weighing). As you enter the program, by selection of one of the themes, a screen opens with graphics representing the chosen scene. Objects can be selected and moved via 'point and click' operation of the mouse and the user can choose to display the data as a graph or table. Three graph options exist (pictogram, bar chart or 3-D bar chart). In addition to this there is a 'simple' or 'totals' display choice. The 'simple' choice displays each item as a separate entry on the graph, whilst the 'totals' option groups identical entries. If the graphing menu is the only one explored then in effect this software is being used as a simple graph-plotting program.

The table facility relates more to a spreadsheet type of package, although dramatically simplified. Again, the 'simple' and 'totals' option, found in the graph menu, is present here. The 'simple' table lists all items selected individually, whilst the 'totals' table groups multiple objects and displays a quantity column. For many users this would still be a far cry from a spreadsheet, although it does provide a simple introduction for young children to presenting data in a table format. The questioning by the teacher and interaction with the pupils would be essential to really develop the potential that this software has to offer – predicting, hypothesising, interpreting, etc. Much of its value would be lost if a pair or small group of children were left to 'play' with it. The modelling aspect of the software has to be appreciated and then the 'what would happen if...?' question can really be explored. Again, this software should be introduced using a large monitor, so that the whole class can join in an interactive exploration of its mathematical possibilities.

## Miscellaneous

Quite often the focus of reviews is on number-based programs and little attention is paid to the other mathematical themes. Several packages are on the market that are dedicated to mathematics as a whole and within these there are sections that specifically address data handling, particularly with the emphasis on using data to interpret and extract information.

**Fun School Maths** (Q, PC) is a collection of 'games', each with three levels of difficulty, set within King Arthur's castle, which is being attacked by Vikings. Merlin, the magician, needs help and as you visit each of the six 'secret rooms' he is present to tell you of your task. The 'Decisive data' room contains displays of pictograms or bar charts (dependent upon the difficulty level selected). The user is asked closed questions about the information within the graph and the opportunity to try again is offered if a mistake is made. Although the target age for this software is 7–11 years, the reading level may be beyond less able or less confident children at the younger end, whilst the scenario may be somewhat immature for Year 6 children.

There is no means by which the teacher can assess how well the pupils managed the task other than observation during use. As a user leaves the 'room' gold coins are 'given', the quantity is supposed to be indicative of how successfully the task has been tackled.

**Maths Explorer** (Granada Learning, PC) provides a virtual world for pupils to explore and discover mathematical problems, investigations and quizzes. There are six zones each containing 'Learn abouts', 'Tell me mores', 'Fact points', investigations and puzzle posts. The data zone is made up of three topics – collecting data, averages and probability. Targeted at Key Stage 2 the 'entry' to the world would undoubtedly attract and capture many pupils' attention, although initial navigation of the zones may prove difficult for some. Direct access to specific parts of the program is possible and a selection of printable classroom materials is also provided. There is a considerable amount to explore within the software as a whole, however it is more manageable if viewed zone by zone. The collecting data investigation allows the user to conduct a traffic survey set in either a city or rural location. Vehicles pass by and the pupil should click the correct icon, in what will form, the table of results. However, the software does not respond to errors, so the resultant table can contain 'unreliable' data. This could be used for discussion. The results are then displayed in a block graph or pie chart and questions appear on the screen to the side of the display. If the pie chart has been selected some of the questions posed cannot be answered because there is no indication of the size of each section of the pie chart. Again, this could be used as a discussion point.

*Use of this software*

If a piece of software contains tasks which the teacher feels could enhance or support pupils' learning, then *how* it is incorporated within the daily maths lesson needs careful consideration. By use of a large screen, some activities may be appropriate to undertake with a class as an example prior to another practical task such as conducting a traffic survey (Maths Explorer). Alternatively, use with a group on which the teacher focuses, therefore promoting discussion and encouraging explanation of methods.

## Conclusion

It is important that the teacher identifies any specific issues related to the use of particular software and discusses these with the children.

The most effective starting point when using data handling software is through whole-class, interactive teaching, where children can see what happens when their collected data is inputted. This data can then be interrogated, especially when key questions to be asked have been identified prior to data collection.

## To summarise

There is a wide spectrum of software to support mathematics. However, much of this may not be suitable for use within the daily mathematics lesson as recommended by the National Numeracy Strategy. That is not to say that ICT should not form part of the mathematics curriculum. It is essential to be selective in the choice of software and how it is to be used to support teaching and meet specified learning objectives.

CHAPTER 4

# Mathematics on-line

*Bob Fox*

As we have seen, one of the main Government initiatives in the late 1990s has been to ensure that all schools, and in theory all pupils, have access to the Internet. It would have been surprising had that not been Government policy, given the extraordinary rate at which the Internet has acquired its status as a fact of everyday life. Funding tied to the National Grid for Learning is ensuring that the necessary hardware and cabling are installed. At the time of writing there is a growing expectation that all schools will create and maintain their own websites, and the software to enable them to do so has rapidly developed and become relatively straightforward, even for the not-particularly-technically-minded. As with other developments in the past, however, the Technological Imperative has been at work, and though all schools may have the capacity to use the Internet, it is not always entirely clear what they should be using it *for* – there is simply the built-in assumption that accessing the Internet must by definition be a 'good thing' (Fox 1997).

In many aspects of daily life the Internet has rapidly become indispensable. This is as true of schools as it is of anywhere else. Increasingly, school administration matters, and particularly liaison with Local Education Authorities and the DfEE and its agencies, are being streamlined through the use of e-mail and the World Wide Web; and it would not be difficult to make out a case for the necessity of Internet access for all teachers, to provide resources, to enable them to keep abreast of new initiatives, and to plan for effective teaching.

Similarly, there would be little opposition to the idea that children of all ages need to know about the Internet, and need some understanding of what it can do; their lives will undoubtedly be significantly affected by it, or whatever it evolves into. Many children have access to it at home, and are completely familiar with sending and receiving e-mail, or conversing with others via a chat room, or surfing the Web in connection with their hobbies and interests. Eventually it may well be viewed as something else on the list of things that everyone just knows about, like using a telephone, changing channels on a television, running a video or finding pages on Ceefax. It was heartening to hear that the government intends to provide computers for children from 'poorer' homes (BBC Ceefax, 28 October 1999).

The use of the Internet in schools is far from unproblematic. There are some major questions to be addressed about, for example:

- the problem of information overload;
- the relationship between information and learning;
- the need to develop information literacy skills (see for example McKenzie 1999);
- authentication of information sources;
- evaluating the appropriateness of reading and content levels;
- relevance of Internet materials to Early Years pupils;
- avoidance of undesirable materials;

and so forth. This list is by no means exhaustive, but a general discussion of the issues falls outside the scope of this book.

As it unfolds, the National Grid for Learning will play an increasingly important role in schools' ICT use, both at national and local levels. At national level, the Secretary of State has offered the frankly terrifying image of hundreds of government-sanctioned lesson plans and worksheets being beamed directly into schools. At local level, there is enormous scope for collaboration. Where LEAs have opted to establish high-speed intranets, giving a permanent connection between schools in a local grid, the opportunities for sharing ideas and resources are immense – though it remains to be seen whether such systems will capture the imagination of teachers in general, or whether they will merely become the haunt of the ICT enthusiasts.

It is curious, therefore, that the two major curriculum policy initiatives that have coincided with the National Grid for Learning, i.e. the Literacy and Numeracy Strategies, have very little to say about the World Wide Web. This is largely because, at present at any rate, the Web has relatively little to contribute directly to the teaching and learning described in the two strategies. Whole-class teaching does not mesh particularly well with what the Web seems to do best. Children will need to be taught appropriate Web skills at other points in the timetable, but the daily mathematics lesson should provide opportunities for children to make use of ICT skills learned elsewhere, and it is not intended that the mathematics lesson itself will be used for teaching those skills directly.

We cannot simply let it go at that, of course. There are some very good websites with numeracy-related content, which can be used one way or another to enhance learning and teaching in the daily mathematics lesson. It would be a futile exercise to list all known sites, as there are many of them, serving slightly different purposes, and the list is added to rapidly and changed frequently. Many of the best sites include extensive links to other sites, and a few examples here should give the reader enough starting points for many hours of happy surfing. This list will be published on the internet from the David Fulton Publishers website www.fultonbooks.co.uk so that links can be clicked directly and can be kept up to date. The addresses here in the printed book were checked immediately prior to the publication of this book, but no guarantees can be given that they will continue to exist (either at the given address or at all) beyond that point.

As with any other topic on the Web, a substantial proportion of what is available is American in origin (e.g. anything with 'Math' in its title), and users should be slightly circumspect about some available materials, for example, worksheets that relate to US currency or non-metric weights and measures.

For present purposes, we will pick 13 sites that all teachers of numeracy should know about. There are other sites containing resources, for which the user has to pay a subscription. They are not included in this list. The amount of worthwhile material that is freely available makes payment unnecessary.

1. Firstly, there is the DfEE Standards site, http://www.standards. dfee.gov.uk/numeracy, from which the whole of the Numeracy Framework is downloadable. If you wish to do this, you must ensure that your computer has an Adobe Acrobat Reader installed, as it is a PDF (Portable Document Format) file. The Reader is available free, and can often be downloaded via links from sites that offer PDF files - in this case, further information can be found at http://www.standards.dfee.gov.uk/about/pdf.

   It is a pity that the document is not available as a text file, as cutting and pasting from PDF files has some unpredictable effects. However, all schools have been provided with the planning grids and each year's teaching objectives on disc, as well as a CD–ROM for the vocabulary. These can be used as text files.

   Anyone interested in the research background to the Numeracy Strategy can access the substantial and detailed annotated bibliography at http://www.standards.dfee.gov.uk/library/research/natnumstrat

2. The Virtual Teacher Centre, which is a central part of the National Grid for Learning, should eventually become an invaluable resource for teaching materials and ideas, though in its first year or so it has proved rather clumsy to navigate, and rather dull and disappointing in its content: http://www.vtc.ngfl.gov.uk/

   An on-line version of the publication *Using ICT in Mathematics* can be accessed at http://www.vtc.ngfl.gov.uk/resource/cits/maths/index.html

3. The Logo Foundation maintains a huge site, with background materials relating to the philosophy and development of Logo, and a large number of links to Logo-related sites around the world. It can be found at http://el.www.media.mit.edu/groups/logo-foundation/index.html

4. The policy of the Numeracy Strategy to teach the whole class together makes it likely that the needs of the most able pupils may not be met unless they have access to good extension and enrichment materials. The Mathematics Enrichment Project, based at Cambridge University, is intended to meet those needs. Its website, NRICH, caters for all age-groups, but has developed an excellent primary section, where users can access a range of problems and puzzles (and their solutions), articles, games, Logo ideas, and other materials intended to inspire and stretch the most able pupils (see DfEE 1998a, para. 60, *Numeracy Matters. The Preliminary Report of the Numeracy Taskforce*). According to the project's mission statement,

> The project aims to establish a permanent national centre for curriculum enrichment to provide mathematical learning support for very able children of all ages. The learning and enjoyment of mathematics will be promoted through an Internet Newsletter and the participation of university students as peer teachers providing an electronic answering service. The centre will offer support, advice and in-service training to teachers, and resources for mathematics clubs.

Space precludes a more detailed examination, but interested readers are referred to the site itself: http://www.nrich.maths.org.uk/primary/index.htm Its aims are at http://www.nrich.maths.org.uk/mathsf/aims.htm and a detailed evaluation report by Libby Jared is at: http://www.nrich.maths.org.uk/mathsf/evalrep.htm

5. The Centre for Innovation in Mathematics Teaching, based at Exeter University, describes itself as 'a focus for research and curriculum development in Mathematics teaching and learning with the unifying aim of enhancing mathematical progress in schools and colleges.'

Its website, at http://www.ex.ac.uk/cimt/ is mostly concerned with secondary mathematics, but it has some interesting puzzles which could be used for investigations, or as extension and enrichment materials for very able pupils. It has an ongoing project, the Mathematics Enhancement Programme, which is developing on-line resource materials for all ages. At the time of writing, none of the primary material is yet available.

6. http://forum.swarthmore.edu/ the Math Forum, based at Swarthmore College in Philadelphia, is a vast site, which succeeds in convincing the reader that simple number work done in kindergarten and complex number work done by professional mathematicians are both part of the same

fascinating endeavour. The site contains sections relating to different age groups, and many puzzles and ideas. There is a particularly useful section on calculation tips at http://forum.swarthmore.edu/k12/mathtips/index.html Dr. Math offers responses to e-mailed queries about mathematics: http://forum.swarthmore.edu/dr.math/

7. http://www.teachingideas.co.uk/mathemat.htm Mark Warner's Teaching Ideas site includes games and activities contributed by teachers. The quality of these is perhaps slightly uneven – some are no more than fairly boring traditional worksheets, but others are quite imaginative, and if you are the school mathematics coordinator it is certainly worth keeping an eye on this site.

8. Kathy Schrock's Guide for Educators, which can be found at http://school.discovery.com/schrockguide/ is a huge annotated list of links to worthwhile sites.

9. 'Games that Interest John Conway' contains some interesting simple games, several of which could form starting points for mathematical investigations and discussions: http://www.cs.uidaho.edu/~casey931/conway/games.html

10. The BBC Education Website contains annotated lists of useful sites for a range of subjects:
http://db.bbc.co.uk/plsql/education/webguide/pkg_main.p_ home

11. http://puzzlemaker.school.discovery.com/ will actually create downloadable puzzles, number squares and mazes to your specification on-line. Some of this material could be used by children within the structure of the daily mathematics lesson.

12. The Association of Teachers of Mathematics (ATM) site is at http://www.atm.org.uk/

13. The Mathematical Association site is at http://www.m-a.org.uk

CHAPTER 5

# ICT in the daily mathematics lesson

*Bob Fox and Sarah Wilkes*

We have considered examples of the main types of software that can be used in the context of mathematics. What we need to consider now is the extent to which they, or any other software, might fit into the prescribed structure of the daily mathematics lesson. Here we are presented with a substantial problem, because on the face of it, relatively little seems to fit the structure. This is paradoxical, given the mathematical bias that pervaded early assumptions about what computers are actually good at, and given the current pressure placed on student teachers and NOF-trained teachers to incorporate the use of ICT into core subjects.

If mathematics software does not fit easily into the daily mathematics lesson, where else should it go? There is so much pressure on curriculum time for other subjects that it is very unlikely that schools will be keen to find extra time for mathematics outside the daily mathematics lesson. The National Numeracy Strategy document talks in terms of fitting it in at break-time and lunch-time, after school and at home – which seems particularly harsh on the most able pupils, who will need access to enrichment materials.

There are of course opportunities to make use of software tools in other subjects. One could use databases, spreadsheets, or graphing programs extensively in science or geography, for example.

And indeed with a little ingenuity pair or group work could be devised within the daily mathematics lesson itself that made use of those tools. For this to be effective, it might be necessary for children to have access to several computers (e.g. in a computer room or suite), as the Strategy recommends that no more than three different group activities should happen simultaneously: 'An aim of the daily mathematics lesson is to keep the class working together and to link but limit to no more than three the number of different activities going on during group work' (DfEE 1999).

It must be emphasised again, though, that learning outcomes within the daily mathematics lesson should be expressed in terms of numeracy, not in terms of ICT; and daily mathematics lesson time should not be used for teaching ICT skills.

There is a different way of looking at it, however. More or less everything we have looked at so far has assumed that computers in classrooms are for children to use, singly or in pairs or groups, or possibly for teachers to use when showing children how to use a particular application. This chapter examines a different approach, which starts from the assumption that, during the whole-class teaching sections of the daily mathematics lesson, the computer is used as a focal point for activities, and the main (but not sole) wielder of the mouse is the teacher. This approach is specifically mentioned in the Strategy: 'you or another adult can make good use of a single computer in the daily lesson by working with the whole class, if the monitor's screen is large enough. An alternative is for you to work with part of the class – perhaps a group of six to eight pupils. As with other ways of teaching mathematics, your role is to demonstrate, explain and question, stimulate discussion, invite predictions and interpretations of what is displayed and ask individual children to come to the keyboard to enter an instruction or a response' (DfEE 1999).

What happens on the screen can be more subtle and certainly more interesting than what conventionally happens on a chalkboard. This approach might not give children first-hand practice at using a computer, but that should not be a principal aim of the daily mathematics lesson anyway. The computer can be used as a means of supporting the dialogue that should characterise a substantial part of the lesson. As an approach, it ensures that the teacher is actively engaged in what happens with the ICT, and the computer is not used as a childminder. What is important about this approach is that it enables the teacher to:

- mediate the activity;
- make crucial decisions about what questions to ask, in what order, and to whom;
- evaluate the appropriateness of pupils' responses;
- make fine adjustments in the process in the light of those responses;
- take account of local and specific factors which might affect the general conduct of the session.

We do not intend to imply that that is the only use to which ICT is put in the classroom. There should still be substantial opportunities, within the daily mathematics lesson and at other times, for children to make use of ICT themselves, much as they have done in the past.

The rule is – keep the technology simple and concentrate on the mathematics. Or rather, keep the technology so simple and straightforward that the mathematical issues do not become obscured or complicated by the technical context in which they are embedded.

One intended spin-off from this approach should be the involvement of all teachers as active users of technology. We saw in Chapter 1 that a substantial proportion of primary teachers are not confident with the use of ICT, and consequently they either avoid it altogether or else they are prepared to allow computers to make decisions about the nature and content of children's learning that should perhaps be theirs. The approach we are exploring here should provide teachers with some successful first-hand ICT experiences of their own. In order for this to be so, the computer application used needs to be:

- simple to operate
- adaptable in use
- sufficiently clear to be visible and readable from a distance (see below).

## Setting up whole-class activities with ICT

Much of what follows does not apply specifically to numeracy teaching, but could be equally applicable to the needs of the literacy hour. If some of the points seem over-obvious, no apologies are offered – even the best teachers can overlook relatively simple points of technique. You might treat what follows as a checklist, or alternatively you might wish to take issue with some of the suggestions. You are allowed to do so as long as that stimulates positive alternatives ('In my situation I would need to do so-and-so instead…'), but approach the suggestions with an open mind, and try to avoid defensive dismissiveness ('That's all very well, but if I tried to do that with my little horrors there'd be a riot…').

Before we turn our attention to the teaching process itself, we must consider some other issues:

- the provision of equipment
- positioning of equipment
- positioning of children
- positioning of the teacher.

### *Provision of equipment*

There is a simple and important truth which must be grasped at the outset. For most really worthwhile whole-class activities, the computer you use does not need to be particularly new, or powerful, or fast – though it would be nice if it had all those qualities, generally speaking, probably, none of them will be specifically required. Good interactive whole-class teaching does not need to rely on whizzy

*By contrast*

graphics or special effects – the pace comes from the teacher, and the fireworks from the excitement generated by the interactivity. We will probably eventually reach the point where Internet access is fast enough to initiate, sustain and support real-time classroom activities, or video-conferencing will enable you to link your class routinely with others elsewhere, but neither of those possibilities is likely to optimise the benefits of good interactive teaching, as we hope to demonstrate below.

An older computer can be put to good use – a 486 or even 386 PC, and Acorn A3000, or even a BBC 'B' or Master 128. The biggest problem you face, when attempting to work with a whole class or large group, is providing a screen image large enough for everyone to see. An older computer with relatively low-resolution graphics can often be connected to a large television screen to good effect, but a large monitor capable of handling the screen resolution and colour requirements of a recent PC is a very expensive item, and it is unlikely that any primary school has a budget large enough to provide one of these in each classroom.

The moral is, if you are acquiring new computers, *do not* let the Technological Imperative bounce you into jettisoning the old ones merely because they are old. There are nearly always good uses to which they can be put, as long as you have physical space for them. Logo, for example, might be considered to gain relatively little from extra speed or memory – some purists would argue that it has actually been made worse by being updated, as it has lost sight of parts of its conceptual background – so, if space permits, why not have a cluster of Logo-only machines? *Do* jettison old computers if they do not work, or if they have become unreliable. Do not allow possession of old computers (particularly broken ones) to be used as an excuse for not acquiring new ones. When you count how many computers you have available, do not include anything over five years old in your calculations. In particular, if you are acquiring a new set of machines to go into a central facility like a computer room or suite, do not let that be the reason for throwing away a perfectly serviceable classroom-based machine.

### Interactive whiteboards

At the time of writing, the ideal presentation device is perhaps the interactive whiteboard. The whiteboard itself is either wall-mounted or else on a stand, and is connected to a computer (conventionally, but not necessarily, a laptop machine), which is connected to a data projector (ideally ceiling-mounted – see below), which projects onto the whiteboard. The user wields a pen-like device, which is in fact a remote mouse, and 'writes' or 'draws' on the whiteboard, or drags projected objects around the board, or uses one of a wide range of other effects to section, highlight, delete or modify whatever is presented on the board. One can present live Internet images alongside text, graphics or whatever, and the possibilities of the technology are huge, if, as yet, largely unresearched. No doubt in the future these devices, or something like them, will be standard issue in all classes – but unless primary teachers are to be dictated to yet again by the Technological Imperative, there is a need for a robust examination of the pedagogical implications and possibilities. It is salutary, though unsurprising, to note that sales demonstrations of whiteboard systems always seem to use as their examples materials that would be appropriate at Key Stage 4 and beyond; though some primary schools are making a tentative investment in their first systems. At the time of writing, interactive whiteboard systems are far too expensive to be a realistic option for immediate installation in all classrooms, though the passage of time and reductions in costs may eventually render this paragraph charmingly naive. Certainly, much of what follows would work rather well with an interactive whiteboard system, though there are a couple of important caveats, which we will note in due course.

## Data projectors

If you cannot afford an interactive whiteboard, but need to enlarge the screen image in order for the whole class to see it, the best option currently is a data projector. The price of these has fallen considerably in recent years, but it would have to fall considerably further before they were anything more than a luxury item for most primary schools. As with many similar devices, there are substantial differences in cost between the cheapest and the most expensive, and by and large you get what you pay for. Certainly, any school contemplating buying one should have it demonstrated in the actual room in which it will be used, as lower-powered projectors struggle to make an impression in a daylight room. On the other hand, many data projectors can be used to project video as well, and it may be that there is a location in the school, e.g. a television room, where a data projector could be permanently located and used on a rota basis. Ideally, if portability is not an issue, data projectors should be ceiling-mounted. This keeps the device out of harm's way, and it also means that the image can be projected over everyone's head, which creates more space for viewing it. Potential purchasers should inquire about the life expectancy of the bulb, as these can be hugely expensive (i.e. in three figures) to replace. If the advice of this book is heeded, and more teachers show a desire to use the computer for teaching whole classes, this could eventually contribute to the further lowering of prices.

## The Cruiser laptop

A versatile alternative to a data projector is a Cruiser laptop computer, which is the device used in the research outlined below. At first glance the machine appears to be a fairly conventional PC laptop computer. What makes it different is that you can remove the screen and place it on an ordinary overhead projector, and thus enlarge your screen image to whatever size is necessary. As long as the overhead projector is well maintained (and many are functioning at only a fraction of their full efficiency due to the collection of dust on the inner glass), the projected image is clear and usable in normal daylight, though it benefits from the judicious adjustment of venetian blinds, and does not cope particularly well in blazing sunshine.

The system used in the research outlined below was equipped with a remote presentation device, connected via infra-red, which allowed the pointer to be moved and clicked, and which also had a range of other special effects, e.g. to highlight or magnify sections of the screen. Additionally it had an infra-red remote keyboard, which also enabled mouse actions and the addition of text where required. Both of these devices enabled greater mobility on the part of the teacher, and enabled children to participate actively in what happened on the screen without having to come to the computer itself, as the remote devices could be passed around the room, and were effective to a range of about ten metres. As reported below, this proved to be not entirely unproblematic in practice.

Some advantages of this system are:

- the cost of the device is a fraction of the cost of an interactive whiteboard system, is substantially less than purchasing a computer and data projector, and is only a little more than one might expect to pay for a comparable conventional laptop machine;
- the availability of removable hard drives, which means that each teacher could in theory maintain their own preferred software and system configuration, at relatively low cost, and devices could be shared among a number of classes;
- excellent portability makes it much easier for classes to share devices, permits teachers to take the computer home to prepare materials, and makes secure storage very much more straightforward.

Some potential disadvantages are:

- classes still need access to overhead projectors – though in many primary schools these have taken on a new lease of life, and are much more in evidence, since the introduction of the literacy hour (you also need a screen on which to project the image);
- the removable glass screen itself is quite fragile, and the equipment needs to be positioned so that there is no possibility that anyone will bump into it;
- overhead projectors generate considerable heat, and, though the screen comes with a fan unit to keep it cool, it can in theory be damaged if the computer is turned off and the screen is left on a hot projector.

*Large monitors*
We have already noted that older computers often work perfectly well when connected to large television screens, particularly where these have SCART

sockets, but the high resolution of recent computers makes this a fairly unsatisfactory option. It is possible to buy very large monitors, but these are rather expensive for what they are, and are often so heavy that portability is not an easy option.

Monitor screens, like televisions, are measured diagonally. For years the standard computer monitor size was 14 inches, but recently more are 15 inches, and when buying new machines it is often possible to specify a relatively inexpensive upgrade to a 17-inch or even 19-inch screen. As a general rule of thumb, a monitor can normally be viewed satisfactorily by one pupil per inch of screen – so a half-class should have no difficulty viewing a large monitor, but a whole class might well find it unsatisfactory, particularly if the text on the screen is small (as is increasingly the case with websites).

In recent years there have been great improvements in flat screen technology, and it is not unreasonable to assume that in a decade from the time of writing we will take for granted that screens are flat, can be any size at all, can be affixed to the classroom wall, and are generally affordable. It is also not unreasonable to expect that by then every pupil will have access to a small device for their personal use, which can be connected (via a lead, via infra-red, or via some other means not yet invented) to the main classroom computer, to the school network, to whatever the Internet has become by then. There are some fairly pressing questions that arise from these assumptions: What are the pedagogical implications? How will it affect what we can teach and how we can teach? Though this book does not claim to have all the answers, it does attempt to sketch out some of the ground, so that primary teachers can think about how they want to employ the technology, rather than having it thrust upon them based on someone else's assumptions about what it is good for and therefore what it should be used for.

## Positioning of equipment

Whether you are using a conventional monitor or some other device, the same principles apply for whole-class teaching.

1. Assuming you are using one computer: mostly, what children need to be able to see is the monitor. This may sound over-obvious, but if there is input to be made from the keyboard, leaving it in the conventional position in front of the monitor can make it harder for a class or group to see what is going on. Place the keyboard to the side of the monitor in such a way that the teacher or pupil typing in can see what is happening on the screen but does not obscure anyone else's view. Using a mouse is perfectly satisfactory if you sit with a rigid flat surface on your lap (a ring binder usually works well).

2.  If the kit is on a trolley: the trolley was the almost universal location for computers for most of their primary school history to date. As we saw in Chapter 1, this was partly because when schools had fewer than one machine per class they needed to be mobile so that they could be shared between classes; and in those schools where security was an issue it needed to be relatively easy to lock them away at night. The increase in the overall number of machines available has meant that rather more are positioned in semi-permanent locations, frequently on work surfaces around the edges of classrooms. For many whole-class teaching situations the trolley needs to be located away from the wall – but be careful that mains leads do not trail across thoroughfares.

3.  If you are working with a group of about six or eight children, it is sometimes a good idea to seat the children at a table, and position the monitor at one end of the table, facing inwards. Place the rest of the computer in such a way that the mouse can be put in the middle of the table, preferably on a mouse mat. All the children should be able to reach the mouse simply by leaning forwards or standing up. The teacher or other adult can be placed almost anywhere at the table, but should be able to reach the keyboard. With careful positioning, the activity you undertake will maintain its collaborative group nature with the screen as a focal point, but children will also be able to write, or use other small equipment, at their place at the table, or take it in turns to use the mouse to alter the contents of the screen.

Generally speaking, whole-class interactive teaching activity is not suitable for use with multiple machines in a computer room or suite, even if it is possible to direct screen output to all the machines. The point is that all participants should be concentrating on one fixed point, and there should be a general sense that all are engaged in a collective discussion.

## Positioning of children

In practice, in many classrooms grouping will mean seating children on the carpet in front of the screen. Where they need to read relatively small text on the screen, and thus need to be fairly close, it is often possible to arrange children at different levels, for example, some sitting on the carpet, some on chairs, and some perched on the edge of desks or tables. However it is done, the intention is that everyone can see the screen, and children's ability to interpret what they see is not inhibited or frustrated by difficulty in deciphering distant text. When one thinks of the awful unreadable handwritten hand-outs run off on a spirit duplicator with which teachers used unwittingly to inhibit children's learning or motivation to learn, and compare them with the computer-generated materials that can now be produced, one realises how far we have come in a relatively short time – we need not reproduce the inadequacies of the past.

As every teacher knows, it is not good policy to pack children together too tightly. Invasion of body-space can make anybody feel uncomfortable, and is a recipe for poking and kicking and consequent loss of concentration. Similarly, no-one likes having their legs squeezed between a table-top and the back of a chair. Children cannot be expected to concentrate hard on the matter in hand if they are physically uncomfortable.

If you have access to a projection device which makes it possible to present a very large screen image, readable from anywhere in the room, bear in mind also that it is not a good idea to position children too loosely either, for several reasons. Firstly, angle of vision does make a difference, and children need to be reasonably straight-on to the screen, particularly when exact pointer or cursor position is important, such as when using Logo. Secondly, it is in the nature of whole-class activity that it encourages collegiality and a sense of identity with the rest of the group, and this is less likely to be encouraged if the class is fragmented. This may vary according to the age of the pupils, and older juniors are more likely to think of sitting on the carpet as rather babyish, and would perhaps prefer to remain in their own places. What matters most is that you should have thought through the type of activity in which the children will be engaged, and should position children accordingly. Will they need to write during the activity? If so, they need something to rest their work on. You can stimulate discussions about problem-solving by prearranging children in pairs or small groups within the whole-class setting.

Children are generally good at changing positions or rearranging furniture efficiently, as long as patterns are well known and there is a degree of predictability.

But, think about positioning in terms of the nature of the activities to be undertaken. Is it all a question-and-answer session? To what extent can children all see each other when there is a high degree of discussion? There is an obvious contradiction between focusing everybody's attention on one small fixed point and expecting them to pay attention to the contributions of others.

### Positioning of the teacher

This is fairly obvious. Because you need to lead the discussion, you must be prominently positioned. Children will need to watch the screen, but will also need to interact with you through eye-contact, gestures and so on, so it is normally advisable to be beside the screen and at a similar height to it – sitting, if it is on an ordinary table, perhaps standing if it is on a taller stand. You will probably need to use the mouse, however, so you will need to make arrangements to be able to do so if you are standing. Occasionally, if you wish to keep everyone's attention on the screen for a sustained period, it makes good sense to position yourself beside, among, or even behind the children.

## Interactive whole-class teaching

You should set up your computer before the session starts, so that you do not take up valuable time and break children's concentration once the session has started. The children should be in a position to see the screen before the lesson gets under way. Unless you intend to use the computer to assist you in the oral and mental starter phase of your lesson (see Chapter 2), it is probably a good idea if you do not allow whatever is on the screen to distract children. If you are using a monitor with accessible controls, you can turn down the brightness until you need to see the screen – or alternatively you could leave the computer running but turn the monitor off.

Once you have completed the oral and mental starter, you should make clear to the children what the objectives of the session are, and how long you intend to spend on any phase of the lesson. From then on, the success of the lesson depends upon the sensitivity and intelligence you bring to bear on the interactions with children. You will need to:

- consider what types of question are most appropriate to any given situation;
- decide who to ask and what to ask;
- maintain eye-contact;
- listen to children's responses;
- ask several supplementary questions to the same child when it is appropriate to do so;
- consider your timing, so that you give children space to respond, but maintain a brisk pace;
- decide how (and what) to praise, and how to keep this in proportion;
- think about how to deal sensitively with tentative responses;
- decide how to deal with frankly wrong responses, without demotivating children;
- keep everyone engaged with the task, regardless of their ability, experience or disposition.

To maximise learning, questions should be pitched at the threshold of children's competence, so that they are challenged, but are just capable of providing a correct response, perhaps with support from you or from others.

None of the above makes any reference to the fact that you are using ICT to support the activity, of course! The expectation is that the ICT will be so straightforward that it passes almost unremarked. There is a slight danger here, however: in Chapter 3 we outlined four functions of ICT, and made it clear that unless you were making effective use of at least one of them you should not use ICT. The Strategy states: 'You should use computer software in your daily mathematics lesson only if it is the most efficient and effective way to meet your lesson's objectives' (DFEE 1999).

In some of the activities described below, the justification for using ICT is not necessarily obvious. For example, where the screen contains a number grid with the numbers covered up, this could have been achieved by other, more prosaic means, like a flannelgraph. The computer is considerably more convenient and reliable, but that alone might not justify its use. The justification comes in the fact that it is easy to select a single grid from a large set of similar grids stored on a disc, and it takes virtually no time to set up, and after numerous interactions with the grid it can be restored to a pristine state more or less instantaneously – so the activity is justified in terms of speed and range. In Cook and Finlayson's (1999) terms, the software used in this sort of activity is passive.

The research we have conducted into interactive whole-class teaching of mathematics has been done using a range of home-made screens for the framework program *My World*. This was chosen because it is in widespread use throughout the country and across the whole of the primary age-range, and because it runs on all major hardware platforms in common use in virtually identical ways.

## 'Mrs Brill Uses ICT for Whole-Class Teaching'

The following script is a fiction, but is based on many actual encounters with children and students. It is intended to be used as the basis for discussion in a lecture, staff meeting or in-service course. Read the text carefully – you might even role-play it – and as you do so, think about the decisions Mrs Brill makes in the order and shaping of questions. As the children are fictitious you cannot, of course, know anything about their previous experience, etc., but decide for yourself, on the basis of the evidence in the text, what the authors intended.

Mrs Brill has a Year 4 class in a fairly average school. She would probably classify herself as a 'late adopter' rather than an ICT enthusiast. She knows enough about ICT to set the machine up, switch it on, and load the program she needs. The children are sitting on the carpet, watching a 17-inch monitor attached to a slightly ageing computer (it doesn't matter what type it is). Mrs Brill has ensured that the children are comfortable, and can all see the screen.

On the monitor there is a *My World* screen containing a large five-by-five grid (Figure 5.2). Each square of the grid contains a large-type number, but the numbers are all covered up by plain squares. Mrs Brill has positioned herself so

**Figure 5.1**   Mrs Brill uses ICT

that she can see the monitor but can also make eye-contact with all the children. She sits with the computer keyboard within easy reach (though she will not actually need to touch it during this activity), and the mouse on a flat board on her lap. The discussion is conducted at a brisk pace.

*Mrs Brill points to the second square in the second row down.*

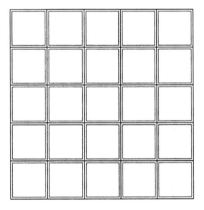

**Figure 5.2**

Mrs Brill:          What number do you
                    think is under there?

*Some children are initially confused, because they have no evidence on which to base a guess; some are perfectly happy to make a blind guess, secure in the knowledge that they cannot actually be expected to know. Some children apply an obvious rule. Timmy's hand goes up.*

Mrs Brill:          Timmy?

Timmy:             I think it's seven.

*Some other children agree.*

Mrs Brill:          Why do you think that?

Timmy:          Well, it's the seventh square. If I start at the top and count, it goes one, two, three, four, five, six, seven...

Mrs Brill:      But do you know for certain that it's seven?

Timmy:          No, that's just a guess.

Mrs Brill:      And it's a very sensible guess – well done. Who thinks they know for certain what it is?

*Several children indicate that they can only guess.*

Mrs Brill:      I think you're quite right. We can't know for certain, because we've got no evidence yet. Timmy's made some assumptions, but he might be wrong. If he is wrong, does that mean he's made a mistake?

*Most children say no. Some are unsure about this.*

Mrs Brill:      Well, let's have a look and see what the number is.

*She removes the cover to reveal the number 28.* (Figure 5.3)

Mrs Brill:      Oh look, it's...

Children:       Twenty-eight.

*She points at the square to the right of it.*

Mrs Brill:      What number do you think that one is, then?

*Several children immediately say 'twenty-nine'. Mrs Brill waits for a couple of seconds before responding. Martin's hand goes up.*

Mrs Brill:      Martin?

Martin:         I think it's thirty-two.

Mrs Brill:      Why do you think that?

Martin:         Because twenty-eight was the seventh square. I think it goes up in fours, because seven fours are twenty-eight.

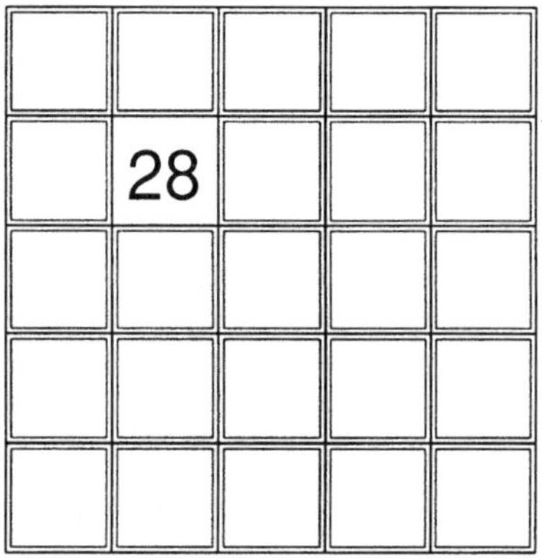

Mrs Brill:      So...

Martin:         So the next square would be thirty-two, because that's four more.

Rachel:         Yes – eight fours are thirty-two.

Mrs Brill:      They are indeed, Rachel. Who agrees with Martin and Rachel?

*Most hands go up.*

Mrs Brill:      Can we be certain, though?

*From the way the question is phrased, children detect that the answer must be 'no'.*

Mrs Brill:      Well, let's have a look, then.

**Figure 5.3**

*She removes the cover to reveal the number 31.*
(Figure 5.4)

| Mrs Brill: | Oh, it's… |
| Children: | Thirty-one. |
| Martin: | Oh I see, it doesn't start with one… |
| Sarah: | Four, you mean… |
| Martin: | It goes up in threes, so it must start with… with… |
| Mrs Brill: | Think about that for a minute, Martin. Mean while, Simon, can you tell me what the next number is going to be? |

*Simon reaches for his fingers, then thinks better of it. His eyes look into the top of his skull, and his head nods slightly three times.*

| Simon: | Thirty-four. |

*Without any more discussion, Mrs Brill removes the cover to reveal 34. (Figure 5.5) Simon looks pleased with himself.*

| Mrs Brill: | Good boy, Simon – well done. Now, who can tell me what number will be below the thirty-four? |

*She points to the appropriate square. Several children's heads start nodding. Katy and Shofiq put their hands up immediately. Anticipating what they have done, Mrs Brill does not ask them – yet. Eventually, Maria's hand goes up.*

| Mrs Brill: | Maria? |
| Maria: | Forty-eight… |

*Several children indicate their disagreement.*

| Maria: | …No, wait a minute….. forty-nine. |
| Mrs Brill: | Let's have a look. |

*She removes the cover, to reveal 49. (Figure 5.6)*

| Mrs Brill: | Very good, Maria. Can you tell us how you worked it out? |

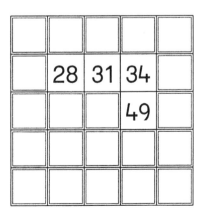

**Figure 5.4**

**Figure 5.5**

**Figure 5.6**

| | |
|---|---|
| Maria: | I kept counting on in threes, till I got to that square… |
| Mrs Brill: | And do you know why it came to forty-eight the first time?<br>Did you just count wrong? |
| Maria: | No, what I did was, I started counting by saying thirty-four again, so I went thirty-four, thirty-five, thirty-six, so I was always one out. |
| Mrs Brill: | So how did you put yourself right? |
| Maria: | I just added one more on to my answer. |

*Martin's hand is up, but Mrs Brill has other business to attend to first.*

| | |
|---|---|
| Mrs Brill: | Did anyone do it a different way? Katy and Shofiq, what about you? |
| Shofiq: | You don't have to keep counting on in threes. There's five numbers in each row, and the difference is always three, so to go downwards you just add on fifteen… |
| Mrs Brill: | Why fifteen? |
| Shofiq: | Because five threes are fifteen. |
| Mrs Brill: | Very good, Shofiq. Is that what you did, Katy? Did anyone else do it that way? |

*A few heads nod. Martin's hand is still up.*

| | |
|---|---|
| Mrs Brill: | Hang on just a moment, Martin – I haven't forgotten you.<br>Let's all do one more first – what's the last number going to be? |

*She points at the square in the bottom right corner. There is a lot of nodding. Several hands go up fairly quickly. Mrs Brill waits until most children have arrived at an answer.*

| | |
|---|---|
| Mrs Brill: | OK, let's see… Laura, what's your answer? |
| Laura: | Eighty-two. |
| Mrs Brill: | Who agrees? |

*Many children do. Mrs Brill reveals that it is indeed 82.* (Figure 5.7)

| | |
|---|---|
| Mrs Brill: | Well done, everyone. Laura, how did you do it? |
| Laura: | I added on thirty… |
| Mrs Brill: | Why thirty? |
| Laura: | Because it's fifteen doubled… and then I counted on another three. |
| Mrs Brill: | Brilliant. Right, Martin – it's your turn again. Can you remind us what you were doing? |

**Figure 5.7**

Martin:          I was finding out what the first number was.

Mrs Brill:       And what answer did you come up with?

Martin:          I think it's ten.

Mrs Brill:       Let's have a look…

*She reveals the first number, which is indeed 10.*
*(Figure 5.8)*

Mrs Brill:       Brilliant! How did you do it, Martin?

Martin:          Well, I counted back in threes from twenty-eight, and I got to ten. Then I checked it by adding fifteen back on, and then another three, and I got back to twenty-eight.

Mrs Brill:       Wonderful! Can everyone see what Martin did? He counted back in threes – is that easy to do, Martin?

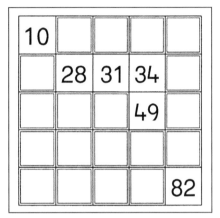

**Figure 5.8**

Martin:          Quite easy, but harder than counting forwards.

Mrs Brill:       And then he checked his answer. How did he do that, Sophie?

Sophie:          He added on fifteen, because that's what a row is worth, then added on the other three to get back to twenty-eight.

Mrs Brill:       Excellent – I think everyone should give themselves a pat on the back, but first, let's all count from the beginning of the grid to the end. Ready, ten…

All:             Ten, thirteen, sixteen… etc.

*Mrs Brill has prepared some worksheets based on a similar grid, which she distributes to children to work on (Figure 5.9). Some children calculate the hidden numbers on their paper-based grid while others use the computer to perform a similar operation, taking it in turns to ask each other what particular hidden numbers might be. In the plenary session, the children demonstrate at the computer how they calculated their answers.*

**Figure 5.9**

In this little scenario there are examples of a range of interactive teaching skills. There are some general points that should be noted:

- Though the activity was clearly planned in advance, and though Mrs Brill exercises a fairly tight control over what happens, the activity could not have run according to a script. Mrs Brill needs the flexibility to respond to children's responses, and to let the conversation go wherever it needs to, though all the time she has her learning objectives in mind, and she has a good grasp of the mathematical issues involved.
- This is intended as an example of the effective use of ICT in interactive teaching, and yet the ICT is almost transparent. The monitor acts as a focus for the activity, and a convenient and efficient way of presenting the problem, but the computer is not behaving as an expert system. It performs no visible calculations, it plays no part in corroborating responses, correcting errors, or congratulating success.
- The use of ICT contributes to the effectiveness of the session because it is specifically geared to the task in hand, quick and easy to set up, clear and uncluttered in the way it does its job, quickly and easily replicable, simple to use, and unthreatening to the technology-shy teacher. In due course, Mrs Brill may feel the need to be more adventurous in her use of software, but that decision is hers – it is not being imposed on her from elsewhere.
- The skills Mrs Brill demonstrates are those of an alert and perceptive teacher; the skill with which she places and phrases questions could not be replicated by a computer.
- Compare this scenario with Mr Hogg's monologue in Chapter 3.

## Research undertaken with a Year 3 class

Of course, the scenario above is a fiction, and perhaps a little too contrived to be convincing. What follows is an account of some real whole-class teaching, following the principles outlined in this chapter.

## Background

Equipment: we invested in a Cruiser laptop computer, using Windows 98. This enabled us to enlarge the screen image via an overhead projector. This computer had a remote mouse or presenting device, and a remote keyboard, both connected via infra-red. The potential advantage of these devices is that the user can move anywhere in the room, and control what happens on the screen, or children can manipulate objects on the screen without having to move from their places. In practice, this did not actually work as well as had been hoped.

Software: As the focus of our research was to be mathematics teaching, the intention was to ensure that the teacher and pupils would require only a relatively low level of ICT knowledge to enable them to complete the task; the technology was to serve as a vehicle or tool within the lesson. *My World* was chosen, as it is simple to operate (basic 'point and click' with the mouse), and once you have used it once you can then run and use any screen. Additionally, *My World* has an open and flexible nature and resources can be designed to make it relevant for almost any task. The screens used were part of a very large set of home-made numeracy materials, and the actual screens used were constructed specifically for the task.

The hardware and software were thus intended to provide:

- a focal point for the activity
- a means of presentation
- a teaching aid
- a resource – screens could be prepared beforehand, and used as the basis for worksheets for group activity.

## Overview of the lesson

The lesson was expected to follow the three-part structure (oral and mental starter, main teaching and pupil activity and the plenary) as suggested in the National Numeracy Strategy. For our research we chose to assume that the teacher would carry out an oral and mental starter and then proceed to use the ICT as part of the main activity and plenary. The screen would act as a focus for the introduction of the main section followed by pupils working away from the screen. The plenary would involve the use of the screen as the children shared their work, misconceptions were dealt with and learning consolidated.

## The school, teacher and children

The school used for our research was a two form entry primary school (Nursery to Year 6) located within a mainly residential, mixed housing (private and council) area of a Midlands LEA. Pupils are drawn from a relatively wide social and cultural mix, with approximately 30 per cent of its intake from ethnic heritage backgrounds.

The teacher, a mature entrant to the profession, was in her second year of teaching. She was a willing advocate of using ICT with children and possessed sound personal ICT capability. Whilst she had an interest in ICT, she was not a mathematician and openly admitted that she did not like maths! Due to her lack of confidence in her own mathematical ability she spent a considerable amount of time on mathematics planning to ensure the lessons she delivered were sound and appropriate to the needs of her pupils.

The pupils participating were a Year 3 class of 28 pupils, who were the upper of two ability sets. Although some children were operating at an above average level for their age, in national terms the majority were average or below average mathematically.

In normal circumstances computer provision in the classroom consisted of one stand-alone machine with a printer. This was usually used for individual work or work in pairs or threes, depending upon the lesson objectives and the software being used. Mathematics software available consisted of data handling and Logo packages. As the standard monitor was the only one available, the computer had never been used as a teaching aid or resource to present mathematics to the whole class.

## The lesson

A series of lessons were planned, all with a 'number' focus. The following is an account of a problem-solving session.

It was expected that teacher–pupil interactions and also pupil–pupil interactions would play a major part in the lesson and opportunities for the children to make suggestions, explain their thinking and methods of reasoning were essential. The Numeracy Strategy objective for this lesson was: 'Solve mathematical puzzles, recognise simple patterns or relationships, generalise and predict. Suggest extensions by asking "What if…?" or "What could I try next?"' (DfEE 1999, section 3, Y3 objectives).

The *My World* screens consisted of some white circles connected by black lines, and two pop-up windows offering the user sets of circular discs containing the numbers 1 to 25. The idea was that users could select any combination of numbers they chose, and then examine the number patterns that could be made by placing the discs on the white circles. Though it would be easy to replicate this activity without the use of a computer, the fact that users had access to a theoretically infinite supply of discs, and could therefore modify the nature of the investigation at a moment's notice, is taken to justify the use of ICT in this context (other activities with the same class, which were not monitored as closely as this one, used number grids and were much closer to the 'Mrs Brill' activity above).

### Introductory activity (whole class)

The teacher set up the screen shown below, the number discs 1–5 were placed randomly beneath the five linked circles, as shown in Figure 5.10. She asked basic closed questions

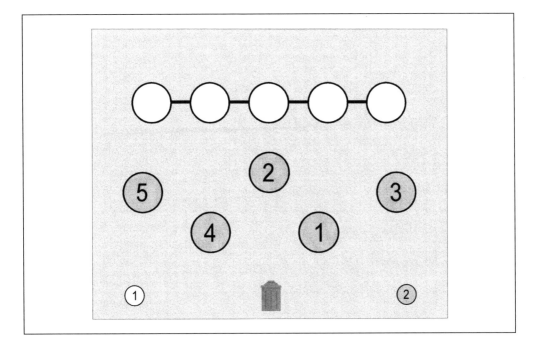

**Figure 5.10**

such as 'What numbers do I have here?', 'Is that the usual order in a number line?' before stating the first task.

*Task 1: rearrange the numbers in the circles so that the difference between any two numbers next to one another is more than one.*
The following is a transcript of the teacher–pupil interaction:

| | |
|---|---|
| Teacher: | What would you put in first? |
| Selina: | One. |

*The teacher moves the 1 to the first circle on the left*

| | |
|---|---|
| Teacher: | What next? |
| Kady: | Four. |
| Teacher: | Why four? |
| Kady: | Four is not near to one. |

*Teacher: (as she moves the 4 into the circle next to the 1) Great. Next number?*

| | |
|---|---|
| Brett: | Two. |

*The teacher moves the 2, so the sequence so far reads 1–4–2*

| | |
|---|---|
| Mark: | Five next. |
| Teacher: | Why? |
| Mark: | Low two, high five. |
| Teacher: | Why couldn't we use the three? |

Rebecca:              Because three comes after two.

Teacher:              Well done.

*The children easily managed this task with the resulting sequence shown in Figure 5.11.*

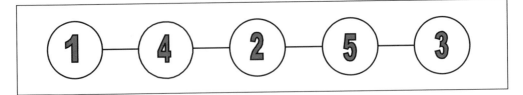

**Figure 5.11**

*The teacher then moved to another challenge:*

Teacher:              If I put the first number in, see if you can arrange the
                     others.

*On this occasion the 5 is placed in the centre circle, as shown in Figure 5.12. The children managed this task successfully, although the teacher had to get the children to specify more clearly where they wanted the numbers to be positioned and at one point the sequence nearly had 4–3–5–. The end result was as shown in Figure 5.13.*

**Figure 5.12**

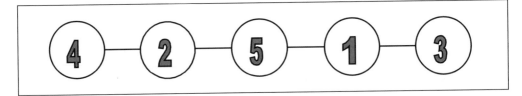

**Figure 5.13**

## Main focus activity (whole class)

At this point the teacher suggested that they play with some more numbers and loaded the next screen as shown in Figure 5.14.

   She described this as a triangle with circles along the sides. One of the number boxes at the bottom of the screen (containing the numbers 1–25) was opened and she asked simple closed questions about the numbers. She told the children that they were only going to use the numbers 1–6 and asked them how many circles were around the triangle.

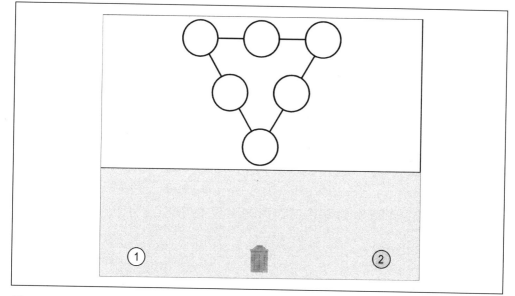

**Figure 5.14**

The task was then stated: 'We're going to use these numbers once only to make the sides of the triangle equal 10'. The pupils' hands shot up at this point. Shakira offered 2, 5, 3 and the teacher asked where and what order they should go in. Shakira proceeded to explain and the teacher then asked if 2, 5 and 3 added up to 10 before asking what should go next (see Figure 5.15).

Amajeet suggested that they should focus on the side with 3 at the top and Rebecca said that they needed to put 1, then the 6. This resulted in the 4 being left to place, but $5 + 4 + 6 \neq 10$ (see Figure 5.16).

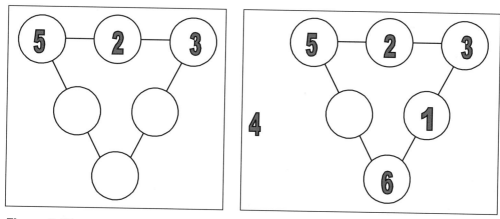

**Figure 5.15**          **Figure 5.16**

At this point Mark, one of the lower achievers, suggested 'put the 4 in the space, then swap the 1 and 6 over so 4 + 1 = 5'. The teacher responded 'Yes, we already have 5, so 5 + 5 = 10'.

As a class, the children checked that each side of the triangle totalled 10 before the teacher moved the lesson on to the next activity which involved the pupils working in pairs at their desks.

### Paired activity

On each table there was a copy of the task, a sheet with the triangle and circles on (the same as the screen they had just been working with), number discs labelled 1–6 and a record sheet.

The activity had been differentiated to cater for pupil needs, with the lower achievers being given more structure as a target number to work to was specified (as shown in Figure 5.17), and the middle and upper having a more open task which was to decide on a target, knowing that 10 did work (as shown in Figure 5.18). The same record sheet was given to each pair (as shown in Figure 5.19).

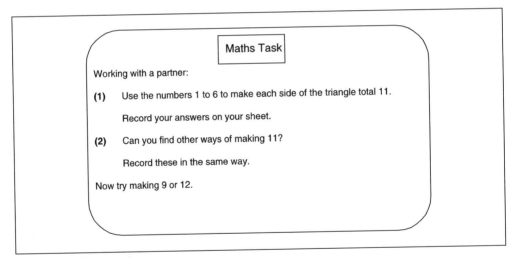

**Figure 5.17**   Task for lower achievers – more structured

### Observations of the pupils working

Some children worked on a trial and error basis, apparently swapping numbers around at random to try and solve the problem. Others showed an appreciation that the order of the numbers did affect the solution. Where pupils had to select the target number the majority tried making 9 or 11 (i.e. one below or one above the target number used as the class activity). Once 9 had been conquered, one pair decided to try making 8 – they reached a point where 6 was left and 'causes

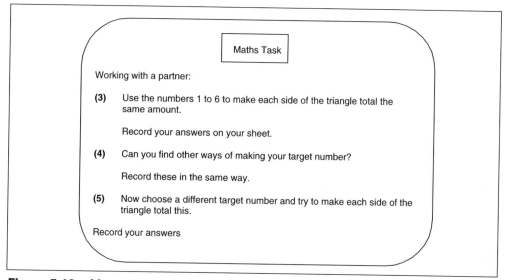

**Figure 5.18**   More open task for middle and upper achievers

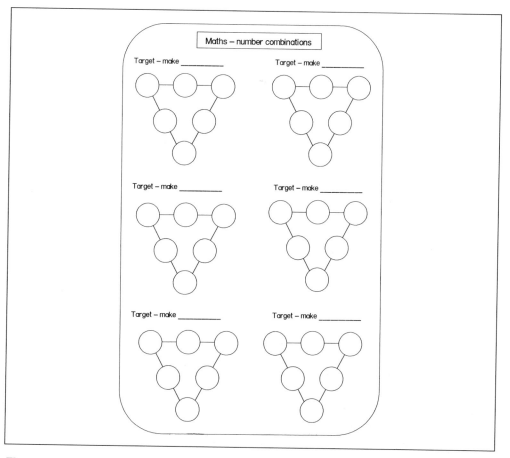

**Figure 5.19**   Task record sheet

problems' (as shown in Figure 5.20). However, neither could explain why 8 was an impossible target, although they were certain it could not be achieved.

Figure 5.21 shows Stacey, with her response to the problem.

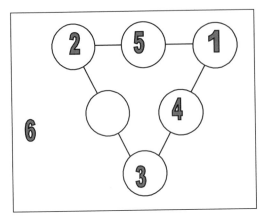

**Figure 5.20**

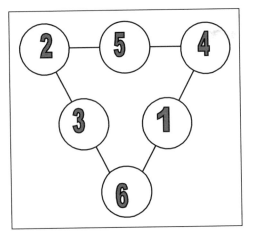

**Figure 5.21**   Stacey's solution to 'making 9'

## The plenary

The teacher drew the pupils' attention back the screen and said that some of them had had to make 11. One pair of pupils shared their solution, shown in Figure 5.22, with the rest of the class. Other alternatives were asked for and the suggestion shown in Figure 5.23 was offered.

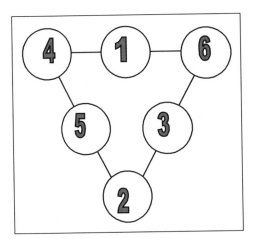

**Figure 5.22**   Solution to 'Making 11'

**Figure 5.23**   Another solution to 'Making 11'

The children were asked to compare both solutions (which was difficult as only one could be viewed at any one time) and share their thoughts. Two main suggestions were put forward:

1. the 1 and 3 were positioned each side of the 6 in both solutions;
2. the need to have smaller numbers near to larger numbers to get solutions that work.

The attempt at making 8 was then discussed and this was shown to be impossible as there would be nowhere to place the 6. At this point the teacher stated that you could therefore only make 9 and above and a method for doing this was shown. Lastly, 12 as the target was explored and shown to work. With more time, the class could have gone on to explore whether 13 was possible (it is not – there is nowhere to place the 1).

## Analysis of the lesson

In terms of the technology the enlarged image acted as a focal point and held the pupils' attention. Whether this was due, at least in part, to the novelty factor of seeing something new and different, only further research would show. However, the teacher did stress that several of the children had very poor spans of concentration and they had notably kept on task. As a means of presentation the teacher felt that the use of *My World* was effective as all the pupils were familiar with its working, having used it since entry to Nursery or Reception, and so they knew immediately how the screen would work. The screens used were simple and clearly laid out which also added to the impact of the presentation.

The technology aided the delivery of the lesson. Movement of the numbers on the screen and the speed at which a new screen could be called up made the process easier for the teacher. Whilst these activities could have been undertaken with paper and blue-tack, or a velcro-style board and pieces, the teacher could move any part of the screen without obscuring the pupils' view and without losing or misplacing any parts; hence, this method was felt to be more manageable.

The main drawbacks with this lesson were:

1. During the plenary, another screen with two triangles with circles side-by-side would have enabled two solutions to be displayed simultaneously; this would have meant that a direct comparison could have been made. This screen was subsequently made.
2. The pupils were not given the opportunity to input their solutions, as in previous lessons they had found the 'Pop' presenter and, to a lesser degree, the remote keyboard, difficult to manipulate. The problems were partly to do with the equipment – it was easy to lose track of the pointer on the screen, and partly to do with the children's unfamiliarity with the device. A

larger, clearer pointer is now available. Therefore, earlier in the study it had been decided the teacher would control the technology. On reflection, it would have been more beneficial, particularly during the plenary, if the children had been able to input their ideas to encourage them to interact with the technology and provide them with the chance to present their ideas and thus have greater ownership of their work. With practice and familiarity with the equipment it was felt that these manipulative skills would be developed, in the same way as control with a mouse is somewhat imprecise when first used, but improves with practice.

## Comment

It is not possible to capture on paper the atmosphere generated by the particular lesson discussed here. The task was straightforward and self-contained, and in general terms it could be considered a success as a maths lesson. Children were well motivated, and their concentration was noticeably better than usual. The intended learning outcomes were achieved, and though it would be difficult to pinpoint precisely which children could now do something better than they could have done it before, observers were left with the feeling that this could have been a sound basis for future work. As an exercise in using ICT to enhance teaching and learning it could also be considered a success, though not amazingly so – but perhaps that is part of the point (see Chapter 6). The case study is, of course, an honest account of a real lesson with very ordinary children. We are all familiar with idealised videos of classroom activity in which a perfect teacher teaches perfectly a class which seems to have only eight pupils, all of whom have straight socks.

# CHAPTER 6

# Conclusion

*Bob Fox*

> The most profound technologies are those that disappear. They weave themselves into the fabric of everyday life until they are indistinguishable from it. (Weiser 1991)

Mark Weiser's vision of ubiquitous computing imagines a world in the near future where personal computers *per se* become unnecessary, because objects have computers built into them, so the technology becomes effectively invisible. Perhaps the key point of this vision is that we will no longer need to fit ourselves into computers' ways of doing things, and no longer feel obliged to conceptualise things in terms of what computers do best:

> There is more information available at our fingertips during a walk in the woods than in any computer system, yet people find a walk among trees relaxing and computers frustrating. Machines that fit the human environment, instead of forcing humans to enter theirs, will make using a computer as refreshing as taking a walk in the woods. (Weiser 1991)

One of the paradoxes with which we have been grappling in this book is why a technology whose founding fathers were predominantly gifted mathematicians should have had so little effect in improving the numeracy skills of young children, so far at any rate. Weiser's vision perhaps gives us a clue: start at the human end, and work outwards from there. If many teachers have been resistant to change, and have not readily embraced new technologies, this is perhaps not entirely because of the reasons into which they rationalise their resistance (though absence of any reliable equipment is a very real impediment). The early adopters, the ones who 'saw the point', have usually managed to overcome the same obstacles that seem to confound the rest. It is not that there is no time to get to grips with the software –

one can learn most of what there is to know about the average primary school software package in about twenty minutes if one has a mind to. Neither is it strictly to do with simple ineptitude with technology - nobody really needs to be *taught* how to use the Internet, you simply click on things (though using it wisely and well is a different matter). Rather, it is to do with the mismatch between the rhetoric and the reality of computers, and the imposition of someone else's idea of how it should all work, and what it is all for.

For many teachers, adopting the structure of the daily mathematics lesson will require a substantial change in teaching style, from being a mere facilitator of someone else's course material to being a very active participant in a continuing dialogue. This will undoubtedly prove challenging for those whose attitude to mathematics is even more phobic than their attitude to ICT. One important difference, however, is that the mathematics schemes on which they may have been dependent were at least designed specifically for use by children. It will probably be the case that being active participants in the daily mathematics lesson will eventually change many teachers' mathematical self-images for the better, as they belatedly discover, or rediscover, a joy in number. In particular, as they reinforce in their own minds the idea that many mathematical problems can be tackled in a variety of ways, they should increasingly find that resources (such as software) that do not acknowledge this are unsatisfactory. Faith in the daily mathematics lesson will endure as long as teachers are able to see real improvements in pupils' mathematical capabilities.

Much educational thinking in recent years has been underpinned by Vygotsky's ideas about learning (Vygotsky 1978), and, in particular, much has been made of the notion of the Zone of Proximal Development (ZPD). This posits that, whatever, wherever and whenever we are learning, we have an area of potential development that we can inhabit, if we are given appropriate support to do so – what a child can do aided today, he or she can do unaided tomorrow. A sensitive teacher of the daily mathematics lesson will always have this in mind, and will not waste children's time with pointless repetition of ideas that are already well assimilated. Note that we do not intend to imply here that one should not provide practice, consolidation or revision opportunities for children – merely that in some cases the actual learning content of mathematics lessons has been depressingly meagre. Done well, whole-class interactive teaching in the daily mathematics lesson provides wonderful opportunities to develop in children the feeling of excitement in learning. The professionalism of primary teachers is closely bound up with their skill in identifying and supporting the learning needs of the children in their care.

Exactly the same points apply to the use of software for mathematics. We should not use it principally so that we can marvel at the brilliance of computers; we should use it to help us develop a better mathematical understanding. The software can be passive, but the user should always be active. In a world which increasingly commodifies education, we find learning represented as something that is done to you rather than something you do – simply sit in front of a computer and it will do mathematics to you. In the context of the primary school, the main justification for the use of a computer should be that it lends support to your learning. In the case of the daily mathematics lesson, much of that learning takes place in the ongoing dialogue between the teacher and the children, and we need therefore to adjust our thinking about how the computer can assist in this. In the previous chapter we made one set of tentative suggestions about how this might work, based on a desire to focus attention on children's learning while simultaneously providing possibly technology-shy teachers with opportunities to engage actively with ICT in a relatively gentle and unthreatening way. We would not wish to leave the reader with the impression that we think that is all there is to it. Just as we anticipate that in the future teachers will feel more confident in their own mathematical abilities, so we expect that ideas about software will also evolve.

At present, the ability of a software package to operate independently of the teacher is often used by publishers as a selling point. We have no specific objection to such software being sold for the home market – indeed, we positively welcome it, as long as the software is well designed and helps to reinforce children's mathematical ideas rather than turn them off – but in the context of the daily mathematics lesson this approach simply will not do. Of course one can set up individual, pair or small-group computer-based activities which are not constantly monitored by the teacher, but they must be related to the whole-class activity, and outcomes from them should ideally be fed back during the plenary. Always keep in mind that learning outcomes should be expressed in terms of mathematics rather than in terms of ICT. Probably the best software to use in this context is either a generic tool like a graphing program or else a 'useful little program' customised to consolidate the particular skill or concept under consideration.

One should also be wary of software that is sold with slogans like 'Makes learning fun!' as this more or less invariably seems to mean that the program is simple drill and practice dressed up with whizzy graphics. In a devastating and funny critique of the idea of 'making learning fun', Stoll (1999) quotes Rudolph Steiner, writing 80 years ago: 'I've often heard that there must be an education which makes learning a game for children; school must become all joy. The children should laugh all the time and learning will be play. This is the best educational principle to ensure that nothing at all is learned.'

This is not simply a killjoy attitude. Candyfloss may be splendid stuff in the right context, but who would thrive on a diet that consisted of nothing else? Learning involves personal engagement with powerful ideas, and very often it is all the more satisfying if it requires a measure of hard graft. It does not have to be dull, but neither should it be unremittingly trivial.

What do we recommend? Here are some suggestions.

We have held back from identifying specific software for specific slots in the National Numeracy Strategy. There are several reasons for this, but the chief reason is that *how* you use software is more important than *what* software you use. Get to know the software at your disposal. Think about the context in which you are going to use it. Apply the criteria outlined in Chapter 3. If it is to be used for whole-class work, consider the organisational issues identified in Chapter 5. Above all else, use it only if it enables you to meet the objectives of the lesson; don't use it merely because it is there or because you think you need to be seen to be using ICT. Do not use it if you could provide the same, or better, mathematical experience without it.

Resist pressures from outside the education system, particularly from people who are trying to sell you something. You almost certainly know more about what your children need than they do. Particularly, do not get lured into a way of thinking about how children learn that does not accord with your own experience as a teacher. Resist the Technological Imperative. Be sceptical, but not cynical.

Be an ICT user. Use ICT tools if they make your life easier or better. Use the Internet, but do not become a slave to it.

The daily mathematics lesson structure brings to the fore a whole range of questions about pedagogy. Much heat and light has been expended on considerations of *what* we should teach, and now the issue is *how* we should teach. Perhaps ICT gives us the opportunity to think in new ways about pedagogy, but we should start that thinking from where we are now, not from where someone else imagines we are, or would like us to be.

Maintain a bouncy enthusiasm, tempered with a healthy scepticism.

# Resources: software and hardware

The following lists are of software and hardware, and their suppliers, mentioned in this book. In brackets, after the supplier, are formats available at the time of writing.

## Software

**Crystal Rainforest**, Sherston (Acorn, PC and Mac)
**FindIt**, Appian Way (Acorn and PC)
**Fun School Maths**, Q (PC: DOS)
**Global**, SIR (PC)
**Graph Plot**, SEMERC (Acorn and PC)
**Hooray for Maths**, Lander Software (PC)
**Junior Pinpoint**, Logotron (Acorn and PC)
**Logo**: a generic term. There are versions available in Acorn, Apple and PC format.
**Maths Frames**, NW SEMERC (Acorn and PC)
**Micro-Smile**, Microelectronics Educational Programme (Acorn)
**Mighty Maths: Number Heroes**, Iona Software (PC and Mac)
**Mighty Maths: Carnival Countdown**, Iona Software (PC and Mac)
**My World**, Semerc (Acorn and PC)
**Pictogram**, CECC (Acorn)
**SuccessMaker**, Computer Curriculum Corporation sold through Research Machines (PC)
**Sumthing**, Resource (Acorn and PC)
The Number Works, Sherston (Acorn, PC and Mac)

## Hardware

**PIP**, Swallow Systems
**Roamer**, Valiant Technology Ltd
**Cruiser V Laptop computer**: enquiries to Presentations by Designs Ltd, 224 Walm Lane, London NW2 3BS, Telephone No. 020 8450 3488

# Bibliography

Ager, R. (1998) *Information and Communications Technology in Primary Schools: Children or Computers in Control?* London: David Fulton Publishers.

Ainley, J. (1996) *Enriching Primary Mathematics with IT.* London: Hodder & Stoughton.

Ainley, J. and Goldstein, R. (1988) *Making Logo Work.* Oxford: Basil Blackwell.

Alexander, R., Rose, J. and Woodhead, C. (1992) *Curriculum Organisation and Classroom Practice in Primary Schools. A discussion paper.* London: DES.

Askew, M. *et al.* (1997) *Effective Teachers of Numeracy. Final Report. Report of a study carried out for the Teacher Training Agency 1995–96 by the School of Education, King's College London.* London: King's College.

Atkinson, J., Spilsbury, M. and Williams, M. (1993) *The Basic Skills Needed at Work: A Directory. A Companion Report to 'Basic Skills and Jobs'.* London: ALBU.

Aubrey, C. (1993) 'Mathematical competencies in young children', *British Educational Research Journal* 19(1), 27–41.

Aubrey, C. (1997) *Mathematics Teaching in the Early Years. An Investigation of Teachers' Subject Knowledge.* London: Falmer Press.

Bagley, M. (1996) 'ILS and the right software', *Educational Computing and Technology* 17(4), 9–18, in Harris, S. (1999) *INSET for IT: a Review of the Literature Relating to the Preparation for and use of IT in Schools.* Slough: NFER.

Baker, C. (1985) 'The microcomputer and the curriculum: a critique'. *Journal of Curriculum Studies* 17(4), 449–51.

Becker, H. (1993) 'Computer experience, patterns of computer use, and effectiveness – an inevitable sequence or divergent national cultures?' *Studies in Educational Evaluation* 19(2), 127–48.

BECTa (1998a) *Primarily IT: Using IT to Support English, Maths and Science at KS2.* Coventry: BECTa.

BECTa (1998b) *The UK ILS Evaluations. Final Report.* London: BECTa–DfEE.

Benzie, D. (1995) 'The impact of our questions on Information Technology policy and practice'. Paper presented at WCCE95, Birmingham.

Blows, M. and Wray, D. (1989) *Bright Ideas Teacher Handbooks: Using Computers Effectively.* Leamington Spa: Scholastic Publications Ltd.

Blythe, K. (1990) *Children Learning with Logo.* Coventry: NCET.

Boaler, J. (1998) 'Open and closed mathematics: student experiences and understandings', *Journal for Research in Mathematics Education* 29(1), 41–62.

Boaler, J. (1999) 'Back to basics or forward to the future?' *Topic*, Spring, Issue 21.

Brophy, J. (1986) 'Teaching and learning mathematics: where research should be going', *Journal for Research in Mathematics Education* 17(5), 323–46.

Brophy, J. and Good, T. L. (1986) 'Teacher behavior and student achievement', in Wittrock, M. C. (ed.) *Handbook of Research on Teaching.* New York: Macmillan.

Brosnan, M. (1998) *Technophobia: Psychological Impact of Information Technology.* London: Routledge.

Brown, M. (1996) 'The context of the research – the evolution of the National Curriculum for Mathematics', in Johnson, D. C. and Millet, A. (eds) *Implementing the Mathematics National Curriculum. Policy, Politics and Practice.* London: Paul Chapman Publishing.

Brown, T. *et al.* (1999) '"Primary student teachers" understanding of mathematics and its teaching', *British Educational Research Journal* 25(3), 299–322.

Bynner, J. and Parsons, S. (1997) *Does Numeracy Matter?* London: Basic Skills Agency.

Clariana, R. (1992) 'Integrated Learning Systems and standardised test improvement'. Presentation at WICAT Users Conference, Sandy, Utah, February, in Harris, S. (1999) *INSET for IT: a Review of the Literature Relating to the Preparation for and use of IT in Schools.* Slough: NFER.

Cockcroft, W. (1982) *Mathematics Counts.* Report of the Committee of Inquiry into the Teaching of Mathematics in Schools under the Chairmanship of Dr W. H. Cockcroft. London: HMSO.

Collis, B. *et al.* (1996) *Children and Computers in School.* New Jersey: Lawrence Erlbaum.

Cook, D. and Finlayson, H. (1999) *Interactive Children, Communicative Teaching.* Buckingham: Open University Press.

Cox, M, (1997) 'Identification of the changes in attitude and pedagogical practices needed to enable teachers to use information technology in the school curriculum', in D. Passey and B. Samways (eds) *Information Technology: Supporting Change Through Teacher Education*, Chapter 10. London: Chapman & Hall.

Crompton, R. and Mann, P. (1996) *IT Across the Primary Curriculum.* London: Cassell.

Cuban, L. (1986) *Teachers and Machines: Classroom use of Technology since 1920.* New York: Teachers College Press.

Davies, J. and Brember, I. (1999) 'Monitoring standards in mathematics in Year 2: an 8 year cross-sectional study', *Internationl Journal of Early Years Education* 7(2) 133–9.

Dearing, R. (1994) *The National Curriculum and Its Assessment: Final Report.* London: SCAA.

Department for Education (DfE) (1995) *The National Curriculum.* London: HMSO.

Department for Education and Employment (DfEE) (1998a) *Numeracy Matters. The Preliminary Report of the Numeracy Task Force.* London: DfEE.

Department for Education and Employment (DfEE) (1998b) *Survey of Information and Communication Technology in Schools, 1998.* London: DfEE.

Department for Education and Employment (DfEE) (1998c) Circular Number 4/98. *Teaching: High Status, High Standards. Requirements for Courses of Initial Teacher Training.* London: DfEE.

Department for Education and Employment (DfEE) (1998d) *The Implementation of the National Numeracy Strategy. The Final Report of the Numeracy Task Force.* London: DfEE.

Department for Education and Employment (DfEE) (1999) *The National Numeracy Strategy. Framework for Teaching Mathematics from Reception to Year 6.* London: DfEE.

Department of Education and Science (DES) (1989a) *Information Technology from 5 to 16 (Curriculum Matters 15).* London: HMSO.

Department of Education and Science (DES) (1989b) *Mathematics in the National Curriculum.* London: HMSO.

Department of Education and Science (DES) (1990) *Technology in the National Curriculum.* London: HMSO.

Department of Education and Science (DES) (1991) *Mathematics in the National Curriculum (1991).* London: HMSO.

Duffin, J. (1997) 'The role of calculators', in Thompson, I. (ed.) *Teaching and Learning Early Number.* Buckingham: Open University Press.

Emblen, V. (1996) 'Bilingual children learning number', in Merttens, R. (ed.) *Teaching Numeracy. Maths in the Primary Classroom.* Leamington Spa: Scholastic.

Fillmore, X. and Valadez, X. (1986) 'Teaching Bilingual Learners', in Wittock, M. C. (ed.) *Handbook of Research on Teaching.* New York: Macmillan.

Fox, R. (1996) Miss Apprehension and Mrs Brill. Micro-Scope (MAPE) No. 48, 8–9.

Fox, R. (1997) The Tyranny of the Technological Imperative, Micro-Scope Information Handling Special (MAPE), 17–18.

Foxman, D. (1998) 'Monitoring trends in numeracy in the United Kingdom, 1953–1995, in *Topic*, Spring, Issue 19.

Foxman, D., Gorman, T. P. and Brooks, G. (1992) *Standards in Literacy and Numeracy.* NCE Briefing No. 10. London: National Commission on Education.

Franke, M. and Carey, D. (1997) 'Young children's perceptions of mathematics in problem-solving environments', *Journal for Research in Mathematics Education* 28(1), 8–25.

Fuchs, L. *et al.* (1998) '"High-achieving students" interactions and performance on complex mathematical tasks as a function of homogeneous and heterogeneous pairings', *American Educational Research Journal* 35(2), 227–67.

Galton, M. (1989) *Teaching in the Primary School.* London: David Fulton Publishers.

Galton, M. and Patrick, H. (1990) *Curriculum Provision in the Small Primary School.* London: Routledge.

Galton, M. *et al.* (1999) 'Changes in patterns of teacher interactions in primary classrooms: 1976–96', *British Educational Research Journal* 25(1), 23–37.

Gipps, C., McCallum, B. and Brown, M. (1999) 'Primary teachers' beliefs about teaching and learning', *The Curriculum Journal* 10(1), Spring, 123–34.

Goldstein, G. (1997) *Information Technology in English Schools. (A commentary on inspection findings 1995–6).* Coventry: BECTa.

Good, T., McCaslin, M. and Reys, B. (1992) 'Investigating work groups to promote problem solving in mathematics', *Advances in Research on Teaching* 3, 115–60.

Gray, E. (1991) 'An analysis of diverging approaches to simple arithmetic: preference and its consequences', *Educational Studies in Mathematics* 22, 551–74.

Harris, S. (1999) *INSET for IT: a Review of the Literature Relating to Preparation for and use of IT in Schools.* Slough: NFER.

Hart, L. (1993) 'Some factors that impede or enhance performance in mathematical problem solving', *Journal for Research in Mathematics Education* 24(2), 167–71.

Healy, J. (1998) *Failure to Connect: How Computers Affect Our Children's Minds – For Better and Worse.* New York: Simon & Schuster.

Heppell, S. (1993) 'Teacher education, learning and the information generation: the progression and evolution of educational computing against a background of change', *Journal of Information Technology for Teacher Education* 2(2), 229–37.

Higgins, S. and Muijs, D. (1999) 'ICT and numeracy in primary schools', in Thompson, I. (ed.) *Issues in Teaching Numeracy in Primary Schools,* Chapter 9. Buckingham: Open University Press.

HMI (1998) *The National Numeracy Project. An HMI Evaluation.* London: OFSTED.

Keys, W. (1998) England's performance in the Third International Mathematics and Science Study (TIMSS): Implications for educators and policy-makers, *Topic*, Spring, No. 19.

Kramarski, B. and Meravitch, Z. (1997) 'Cognitive-metacognitive training within a problem-solving based Logo environment', *British Journal of Educational Psychology* 67, 425–45.

Leung, F. K. S. (1995) 'The mathematics classroom in Beijing, Hong Kong and London', *Educational Studies in Mathematics* 29, 297–325.

Lewis, A. (1997) 'Integrated Learning Systems (ILS) and pupils with SEN: what have we learned so far?', *Computer Education* 90, 15–6.

Linchevski, L. and Kutscher, B. (1998) 'Tell me with whom you're learning and I'll tell you how much you've learned: mixed-ability versus same-ability grouping in mathematics', *Journal for Research in Mathematics Education* 29(5), 533–54.

Loveless, A. (1995a) 'IT's another plate to spin: primary school mentor's perceptions of supporting student experience of information technology in the classroom', *Journal of Information Technology for Teacher Education* 4(1), 39–50.

Loveless, A. (1995b) *The Role of IT – Practical Issues for the Primary Teacher*. London: Cassell.

Luxton, R. G. and Last, G. (1997) *Under-achievement and Pedagogy. Experimental reforms in the teaching of mathematics using Continental approaches in schools in the London Borough of Barking and Dagenham*. London: National Institute of Economic and Social Research.

Luxton, R. G. and Last, G. (1998) 'Under-achievement and Pedagogy. Experimental reforms in the teaching of mathematics using Continental approaches in schools in the London Borough of Barking and Dagenham', *Teaching Mathematics and its Applications* 17(1), 1–11.

Mansell, W. and Bowen, L. (1999) 'Giant leap for maths-kind', *Times Educational Supplement,* 20 August.

McCaslin, M. *et al.* (1994) 'Gender composition and small-group learning in fourth-grade mathematics', *The Elementary School Journal* 94(5), 467–82.

McClees, D. and Fitch, D. (1995) 'The case for classic Logo', *Logo Update* 4(1), http: el.www.media.mit.edu/groups/logo-foundation/LU/v4n1.html

McFarlane, A. (ed.) (1997) *Information Technology and Authentic Learning*. London: Routledge.

McKenzie, J. (1998) 'The information literate school community', *From Now On – The Educational Technology Journal* 8(1), http://www.fno.org/

McKenzie, J. (1999) 'Reaching the reluctant teacher', *From Now On – The Educational Technology Journal* 8(1), http://www.fno.org/

Mercer, N. and Wegerif, R. (1998) 'Is "exploratory talk" productive talk', in Littleton, K. and Light, P. *Learning with Computers: Analysing Productive Interactions*. London: Routledge.

Miller, L. and Olson, J. (1994) 'Putting the computer in its place: a study of teaching with technology', *Journal of Curriculum Studies* 26(2), 121–41.

Millet, A. and Johnson, D. C. (1996) 'Solving teachers' problems: the role of the commercial mathematics scheme', in Johnson, D. C. and Millet, A. (eds) *Implementing the Mathematics National Curriculum Policy. Politics and Practice*. London: Paul Chapman Publishing.

Mills, C. J., Ablard, K. E. and Gustin, W. C. (1994) 'Academically talented students' achievement in a flexibly paced mathematics program', *Journal for Research in Mathematics Education* 25(5), 495–511.

Monteith, M. (ed.) (1998) *IT for Learning Enhancement*. Exeter: Intellect Books.

Nattiv, A (1994) 'Helping behaviors and math achievement gain of students using cooperative learning', *The Elementary School Journal* 94(3), 285–97.

NCET (1994) *Information Technology Works: stimulate to educate*. Coventry: NCET

NCET (1996) *Whole School Development of Higher Order Information Handling Skills* http://vtc.ngfl.gov.uk/resource/cits/primary/skills.html

NCET (1997) *Primary Mathematics with IT*. Coventry: NCET.

Newstead, K. (1998) 'Aspects of children's mathematical anxiety', *Educational Studies in Mathematics* 36, 53–71.

Nicol, C. (1999) 'Learning to teach mathematics: questioning, listening and responding', *Educational Studies in Mathematics* 37, 45–66.

Noss, R. (1991) 'The social shaping of computing in mathematical education', in Pimm, D. and Love, E. (eds) *Teaching and Learning School Mathematics*. London: Hodder and Stoughton.

O'Duill, M. (1997) 'Understanding our instrument of representation', in Passey, D. and Samways, B. (eds.) *Information Technology: Supporting Change Through Teacher Education,* Chapter 37. London: Chapman & Hall.

OFSTED (1998) *The Annual Report of her Majesty's Chief Inspector of Schools. Standards and Quality in Education 1996–7*. London: OFSTED.

OFSTED (1999) *Primary education: a Review of Primary Schools in England, 1994–1998.* London: OFSTED.

Owen, T. M. (1999) 'Learning using computers … the need for an educational standard', *Education Technology and Society* 2(4), http://ifets.ieee.org/periodical/vol_4_99/v_4_99.html

Papert, S. (1980) *Mindstorms.* Brighton: Harvester Press.

Papert, S. (1993) *The Children's Machine: Rethinking School in the Age of the Computer.* Hemel Hempstead: Harvester Wheatsheaf.

Passey, D. and Samways, B. (eds) (1997) *Information Technology: Supporting Change Through Teacher Education.* London: Chapman & Hall.

Perry, M., VanderStoep, S. W. and Yu, S. L. (1993) 'Asking questions in first-grade mathematics classes: potential influences on mathematical thought', *Journal of Educational Psychology* 85(1), 31–40.

Philipp, R. *et al.* (1994) 'Conceptions and practices of extraordinary mathematics teachers', *Journal of Mathematical Behavior* 13, 155–80.

Postman, N. (1985) *Amusing Ourselves to Death.* London: Heinemann.

Postman, N. (1993) *Technopoly: The Surrender of Culture to Technology.* New York: Viking.

Prais, S. and Luxton, R. (1998) 'Are the proposed reforms of numeracy teaching sufficient for success?', *Teaching Mathematics and Its Applications* 17(4), 145–51.

Putnam, R. T. *et al.* (1992) 'Teaching mathematics for understanding: discussing case studies of four fifth-grade teachers)', *The Elementary School Journal* 93(2), 213–28.

Reynolds, D. (1996) *Worlds Apart? A Review of International Surveys of Educational Achievement involving England.* London: OFSTED.

Romberg, T. A. and Carpenter, T. P. (1986) 'Research on teaching and learning mathematics: two disciplines of scientific inquiry', in Whittrock, M. C. (ed.) *Handbook of Research ion Teaching.* New York: Macmillan.

Rowland, T. (1995) 'Between the lines: the language of mathematics', in Anghileri, J. (ed.) *Children's Mathematical Thinking in the Primary Years. Perspectives on Children's Learning.* London: Cassell.

Russell, T. (1995) 'IT in education – where have we gone wrong?', *Computer Education* 81, 2–4.

Ruthven, K. and Chaplin, D. (1997) 'The calculator as a cognitive tool: upper primary pupils tacking a realistic number problem', *International Journal of Computers for Mathematical Learning* 2, 93–124.

Ruthven, K., Rousham, L. and Chaplin, D. (1997) 'The long term influence of a "calculator-aware" curriculum on pupils' mathematical attainments and attitudes in the primary phase', *Research Papers in Education* 12(3), 249–82.

Sawyer, A. (1993) *Developments in Primary Mathematics Teaching.* London: David Fulton Publishers.

Shuard, H. *et al.* (1991) *Calculators, Children and Mathematics,* The PrIME Project. Hemel Hempstead: Simon & Schuster.

Smith, H. (1999) *Opportunities for Information and Communication Technology in the Primary School.* Stoke on Trent: Trentham Books.

Somekh, B. and Davies, R. (1991) 'Towards a pedagogy for Information Technology', *The Curriculum Journal* 2(2), 153–70.

Somekh, B. and Davis, N. (eds) (1997) *Using Information Technology Effectively in Teaching and Learning.* London: Routledge.

Stevenson, D. (1996) *Information and Communications Technology in UK Schools: an Independent Inquiry.* London: Independent ICT in Schools Commission.

Stoll, C. (1999) *High Tech Heretic: Why Computers Don't Belong in the Classroom.* New York: Doubleday.

Straker, A. (1989) *Children Using Computers*. Hemel Hempstead: Simon & Schuster.

Straker, A. (1999) 'Star role and support cast', *Times Educational Supplement*, 2 July, page 20.

Sutherland, R. (1993) 'Connecting theory and practice: results from the teaching of Logo', *Educational Studies in Mathematics* 24, 95–113.

Tabberer, R. (1997) 'Teachers make a difference: a research perspective on teaching and learning in primary schools', *TOPIC* (NFER), Issue 18, No. 2.

Thompson, I. (1997) 'The early years number curriculum today', in Thompson, I. (ed.) *Teaching and Learning Early Number*. Buckingham: Open University Press.

Thompson, I. (ed.) (1999) *Issues in Teaching Numeracy in Primary Schools*. Buckingham: Open University Press.

Thwaites, A. and Jared, L. (1997) 'Understanding and using variables in a variety of mathematical contexts', in McFarlane, A. (ed.) *Information Technology and Authentic Learning*, Chapter 4. London: Routledge.

Turkle, S. (1997) 'Seeing through computers: education in a culture of simulation. *The American Prospect* 31, 76–82 (http://epn.org/prospect/31/31turkfs.html)

Underwood, J. (1996) 'Are Integrated Learning Systems good for teachers too?', *Journal of Information Technology for Teacher Education* 5 (3), 207–18.

Underwood, J. (1997) 'The role of integrated learning systems', *Topic* 18, Autumn.

Underwood, J. and Brown, J. (eds) (1997) *Integrated Learning Systems. Potential into Practice*. Oxford: Heinemann.

Underwood, J. and Underwood, G. (1990) *Computers and Learning*. Oxford: Basil Blackwell.

Veen, W. (1993) 'The role of beliefs in the use of information technology: implications for teacher education, or teaching the right thing at the right time', *Journal of Information Technology for Teacher Education* 2(2), 139–53.

Verschaffel, L. and De Corete, E. (1993) 'A decade of research on word problem solving in Leuven: theoretical, methodological, and practical uutcomes', *Educational Psychology Review* 5(3), 239–56.

Vygotsky, L. (1978) *Mind in Society: The Development of Higher Psychological Processes*. Cambridge, Mass.: Harvard University Press.

Walton, D. (1984) 'Structured reinforcement', in Jones, R. (ed.) *Micros in the Primary Classroom*. London: Edward Arnold.

Wegerif, R. and Scrimshaw, P. (eds) (1997) *Computers and Talk in the Primary Classroom*. Clevedon: Multilingual Matters.

Weiser, M. (1991) 'The computer for the 21st century', *Scientific American*, September, 94–104. See also http://www.ubiq.com/hypertext/weiser/Ubi Home.html

Wild, M. (1996) 'Technology refusal: rationalising the failure of student and beginning teachers to use computers', *British Journal of Educational Technology* 27(2), 134–43.

Wiliam, D. (1998) Relevance as MacGuffin in mathematics education', *Chreods*, Issue 12. http://s13a.math.aca.mmu.ac.uk/Chreods/Issue_12/Wiliam.html

Whitburn, J. (1995) 'Teaching mathematics in Japan', *Oxford Review of Education* 21(3), 347–60.

Whitebread, D. (1997) 'Developing children's problem-solving: the educational uses of adventure games', in McFarlane, A. (ed.) *Information Technology and Authentic Learning: Realising the Potential of Computers in the Primary Classroom*. London: Routledge

Wood, T. and Sellers, P. (1997) 'Deepening the analysis: longitudinal assessment of a problem-centered mathematics program', *Journal for Research in Mathematics* 28(2), 163–86.

Zack, V. (1999) 'Everyday and mathematical language in children's argumentation about proof', *Educational Review* 51(2), 129–46.

# Index

difficult to pick out exactly what you took from your dad – for better or worse. A good start is to ask your partner. Even if she has not told you before, she will have an insight into the similarities between you and your family, and the traits you have picked up from your father, whether you like what she has to say or not!

Either way, this issue is going to take up considerable thinking time, something of which you probably don't have a lot right now. But it is essential to have some sort of guiding principles to hold onto as you go through the fatherhood experience. Not a plan that is rigid and intimidating, but guidelines that will develop as you progress, to provide some solid grounding and structure in your children's lives, that they can work from and grow their own characters.

One way of starting to think about this is to write down the key qualities that you would like to see in your children as adults. Then write a list of your own qualities. How do they compare? At this stage you may want to risk ridicule by showing the lists to your partner and asking whether she agrees. (Maybe she should write her own lists?) If your lists are a reasonable match, then you are already on the right track. But now take the list of your qualities and write down how you demonstrate each of those qualities to your child in daily life.

This is the difficult part.

Most of us assume that we are good people and our children will turn out the same. But maybe we should look at our behavior a bit more closely. Children cannot tell the difference between right and wrong, and cannot understand irony. Adults can see through their less attractive habits, and take themselves as a whole package, balancing the good and the bad.

Knowing that we mean well, even if we do not always show it. Children, on the other hand, will see us doing things, assume they are good, and adopt them. For example, recent research on bullying in schools suggests that the bullies are used to being frightened and bullied at home by their parents, and naturally replicate that behavior when they are interacting with other children.

So when it comes to influencing your children, it's no good just having a list of guiding principles, you have to live up to those standards and let your children see you doing it. If this all seems too theoretical at the moment, then one area where you can achieve quick, practical benefits for you and your child, is by looking at the way that you and your partner interact as a couple. Your child is going to be heavily influenced in the way he conducts relationships by the way that his parents behave, so aim to keep any difficult stuff private but let your child see, and take part in, the caring, affectionate and communicative relationship that you and your partner share.

# Matters of discipline

The way that you guide and discipline your toddler will inevitably affect the way that he grows up and behaves as an older child and adult. Too much authoritarian discipline can leave him unable to make decisions for himself in later life. On the other hand, too little discipline at an early age can mean that he fails to develop any real self control or willingness to accept responsibility for his actions. So it makes sense to follow a more flexible route, which falls somewhere between those two extremes. This approach embraces firm rules, but the discipline is accompanied by explanation, discussion and a degree of independence for your child. He will grow up in a supportive environment in which his needs are respected. Hopefully, this path will lead to a self-reliant, self-controlled and socially aware older child, and eventually an adult of similar qualities.

## THE GOLDEN RULES

**Be consistent in your approach** It's very important that you set reasonable limits and stick to them. Your child will become confused and frustrated if he is allowed to do something one day but is reprimanded for doing the same thing on the following day. Both parents must agree a strategy on discipline and avoid giving your child the chance to manipulate one parent against the other.

**Give your child clear guidelines** Be specific about the rules rather than making vague statements. Explain why he is being disciplined, for example because he hit someone again after you had told him to stop. And don't punish him twice – if he has already been told off by one parent he should not be disciplined again for the same misdemeanour.

**Use language consistently** There are many ways of saying the same thing but your child will probably assume they all have different meanings and become confused. For example, all of these words

## DIFFERENT TYPES OF PUNISHMENT

**Reprimand** Children are keen to please their parents, so a stern telling off when they are doing, or have done, something naughty, can be very effective. But it will only work if used sparingly and with conviction. Constantly telling off your child for the slightest misdemeanour will have a negative effect and he will simply stop listening. When reprimanding your child:

- Make sure you have his full attention. Look him in the face by bending down to his level or sitting him up on a chair.
- Your voice should be firm and confident. Keep your words short and to the point, making it clear why you are unhappy.
- Point out the consequences of continued bad behaviour.
- Check that he has understood what you have said.

**Time out** This is a simple, unemotional and effective way of correcting poor behaviour, or removing your child from a deteriorating situation. When he misbehaves, remove him to a separate room and tell him to sit quietly on a chair that he can climb onto himself. Tell him why he is having 'time out' and leave him there, for about a minute for each year of his age. Ideally, the room should be quiet and unstimulating, such as a hallway. If he leaves the room before the time is up, calmly take him back to the

and phrases essentially mean 'No': wait, stay, don't, don't move, don't do that, come back, leave it alone, stop. Try to agree with your partner the simple commands that you want to use and then do so consistently to achieve the right response from your toddler. But remember that over-use of any one command will eventually lead to indifference.

**Praise your child** When he behaves well, make sure you give your child credit, rather than only commenting on negative behaviour. Positive reinforcement of good habits is the best way to improve his behaviour over the long term.

**Don't make empty threats** Only threaten punishments that you know you will carry out. For example, saying that he will never be allowed to eat chocolate again is a threat that has zero chance of being implemented. Your toddler will soon realise that you do not mean what you say and discipline at any level will become difficult to enforce.

**Give your child a chance** Make sure he has the opportunity to try alternative behaviour before you punish him, or give him time to respond to your request. If he's kicking a chair, for example, suggest that he goes outside and kicks a ball. Tell him you will count to ten, and warn him of the consequences if he fails to respond.

**Make up with your child afterwards** Once you have disciplined your child, let him know that you still love him as much as ever, and then move on to other things.

chair. Repeat as necessary until the time is served, avoiding any discussion. Once the time is up, give him a cuddle and forget the incident. As with all disciplinary techniques, over-use will limit the effect.

**Smacking** Most parents are tempted to spank their child at some point, and some believe that a short smack is an effective way of dealing with bad behaviour. It should only ever be used as a last resort, if at all. Smacking is forbidden in some countries, and even if it's not illegal, there are very strong reasons why it should be avoided. Firstly, you could injure your child, or lose control of yourself. Secondly, smacking is usually ineffective because the child becomes used to

it. And thirdly, it can induce aggressive behaviour in your child, because he thinks that it must be acceptable if you are doing it to him.

If you do smack your child, it should be done immediately and sparingly – a sharp tap on the hand when he is heading towards danger – and when all other tactics have failed. Only your hands should be used and only one smack given.

## Tackling bad behaviour

Children need boundaries to help them regulate their behaviour. Knowing what's expected of them and how far they can go will make them feel safe and secure. Guidelines need to be set and bad behaviour controlled. But a toddler is only just starting to learn how to control his body and behaviour, so any discipline from you must be appropriate to your child's age and understanding.

Even when your child is old enough to understand the rules, it is only normal if he tries to push the limits, just to see what he can get away with. But often you can head off potential conflict by anticipating bad behaviour and removing your child from the scene, being aware of trigger factors, ignoring minor offences and trying to avoid saying 'No' repeatedly.

It can be very easy for modern dads to slip into habits more usually associated with the traditional, disciplinarian father figure. We are probably more inclined to take a tougher line than our partners, due to our own male upbringings. This is reinforced by the natural instinct to help our partner by taking control of the situation, and at first it seems to work. Your toddler may be ignoring your partner's complaints but a stern reprimand from you surprises him and he responds as you wish. However, the impact soon wears off and each night you are left shouting ever louder to get your way. Where will it end?

Discipline within the family is about teamwork – and hard work. You cannot hope to resolve your son's disciplinary problems with a quick fix each evening. If your partner is caring for him through the day, then she is the major influence on his behaviour. But it's not her fault that she's run out of options because, as you know, looking after a toddler is a tough job.

The key to solving the problem is to agree a concerted approach that works for you both, even though it will require a lot of self-discipline from yourselves, and will inevitably take longer to implement than the miracle cure that you (and all other parents!) are looking for.

Try to discuss it at the weekend when there is less pressure, and make gradual changes during the day and night to eventually bring about the desired effect. It has to be a joint approach, applying consistent boundaries with agreed strategies, 24 hours a day. Even then, your toddler will still find gaps, and the end of the day is always going to be stressful, but at least you're on the right track. And at the times when you wonder whether it's worth all the effort, just remind yourself why you're doing it: because you want your son to respect you, not live in fear of you.

**WE NEED TO TALK** | ABOUT DISCIPLINARY MATTERS

Why are you always left feeling like the bad guy? You get home from work and the house is in chaos. Your son is running riot and your partner's in tears. You complain that she needs to enforce more discipline, and then shout at your son when you can't get him to sleep. Your partner then shouts at you for shouting at your son. By the time the weekend comes, she's had enough of his tantrums so leaves the discipline to you. But then you feel that the little time you have with your son is spent arguing with him. Does that sound familiar? The first thing you need to do is sit down quietly with your partner and try to take a detached overview of the situation. The only way to start tackling the problem is through teamwork. Work out a simple strategy, with a start date. Stick to it, and only change the plan in agreement with your partner.

## Tackling tantrums

Most children between the ages of 18 months and three years exhibit uncontrollable rages or temper tantrums occasionally – but some have them more frequently than others. Strong-willed or determined children, for example, have more of them than the placid and easy-going types. With some children a tantrum may be a short outburst of rage that soon blows over but for others it may last for some time, with the child lying on the ground thrashing his arms, kicking and screaming, throwing things or holding his breath.

Having an occasional temper tantrum may actually be good for your child's emotional development. It can release his pent up frustration, and teach him that feeling anger is normal, but that its expression needs to be controlled. It also means that your child has energy and assertiveness that will stand him in good stead later on. But too many tantrums are exhausting for the whole family and can develop into antisocial behaviour. So if your child has tantrums frequently, try to work out the reasons why and, as far as possible, avoid these trigger situations (see causes, below).

### Breath holding

It is not unusual for a toddler to hold his breath when in a temper. The child becomes redder and redder and then turns blue or may turn white. The breathing usually starts again at this stage, but sometimes the child goes stiff or floppy or may even pass out. Seeing your child holding his breath is very frightening, but highly unlikely to harm him. If he becomes unconscious after breath-holding, check with your doctor to exclude any medical cause.

> **WE NEED TO TALK** | ABOUT SPANKING
>
> If you manage to avoid spanking your child during the toddler years then you are doing very well. You will certainly come close at times, and it's an issue that you need to discuss with your partner before your child reaches the age where it's a possibility. You need to know how each other feels about the issue, and discuss ways that you can avoid reaching breaking point. If it happens, you will undoubtedly feel guilty afterwards and should talk through the incident, without attaching blame, to hopefully learn from it. Also make sure that if one of you does spank your child, you apologise to him, give him a cuddle and tell him how much you love him.

Otherwise, difficult though it is, ignore your child when he holds his breath – don't slap him or pour cold water on him. In the unlikely event that he becomes briefly unconscious, watch him carefully, but move away as soon as he starts to come round.

### Head banging

Between the ages of one and two, if a child does not have his own way or gets into a temper tantrum, he may bang his head against the wall or floor. Although you will worry that your child will hurt himself, injury is rare. If he is otherwise normal, head banging is nothing to worry about and best ignored. Some children also head bang before going to sleep, or if they are tired or bored.

### Causes of temper tantrums

- *Attention seeking behaviour* Toddlers love to be the centre of attention, and throwing a tantrum may be one way of achieving this.
- *Frustration* This may result if your child is not allowed to do something he wants to do, he is unable to do something due to limited capabilities, or if he is made to do something he does not want to do. Pick your battles, and don't fight over small things

that do not really matter, such as objecting to him wearing odd socks or not letting him pick what t-shirt to wear.

- *Imitation*  He may see and copy another child or adult having a tantrum.
- *Blackmail*  He may use a tantrum as a device to get his own way.
- *Tiredness*  Tantrums are more common if a child is tired or overexcited.
- *Hunger*  Children need to eat regularly, and if mealtimes are too far apart your child may get hungry. Make sure he has some nourishing snacks in-between meals.
- *Inconsistency*  Allowing him to do some things, but not others, without any clear guidelines, or one parent saying 'Yes', and the other 'No', is confusing and frustrating for your toddler.
- *Unrealistic expectations*  Don't expect too much from your toddler; build in rest time during the day. If too many activities are packed into a day, or you expect him to come shopping when he's been busy at playschool, then an explosion is more likely.

**Dealing with tantrums**

As far as possible, try to identify trigger situations and avoid them. But if your child does throw a tantrum, try to keep calm and remember that, in time, he will get over this difficult phase.

As he grows older you will be able to talk more about angry feelings, and ways of coping with them. Meanwhile, don't lose your own temper or give in, and don't try to deal with the tantrum using bribes, smacking or threats. Try the following instead:

- *Distract*  Point out of the window at something or suggest going to the park.
- *Ignore*  If your child does not have an audience, he cannot perform. Put him in a different room until the tantrum is over or, if he is safe, you leave the room. If out in public, decide whether to stay put until the tantrum blows over and ignore any disapproving comments or looks, or whether to physically remove him from the scene with the least possible fuss. If your child is kicking and screaming, move any potentially dangerous objects out of his reach, so that he cannot hurt himself.
- *'Angry toys'*  Provide your child with alternative outlets for anger and frustration. Toy drums or other musical instruments may help him work out his feelings and channel them in constructive ways, as will physical activities such as riding a tricycle. You also can encourage him to

**WE NEED TO TALK** | ABOUT STRESS BUSTING

Your partner is becoming increasingly stressed by your toddler's difficult behaviour – regular tantrums and constant whining in between. This is actually normal behaviour as your child struggles to come to terms with the world and battles with his own limitations. But that doesn't make it any easier to deal with. The build-up of stress through the day means that your partner is more likely to react badly, and in turn the child becomes more tearful and demanding. It's a vicious circle but you can help your partner lessen the effects. For a start, encourage her to have a complete break from home life by going away for a night or weekend with a friend. Hopefully she will come back feeling refreshed, and more able to take an objective view of the situation. Help her to identify the most problematic periods in the day when she really needs to take a 'time out'. Anything she can do to break the build-up of stress levels will help avoid her feeling overwhelmed towards the end of the day.

express himself through colouring, drawing or painting pictures.

- *Join in*  If your child is shouting, accompany him for a while, then gradually lower your voice – your child will probably copy you until you are both whispering. This will help show your child that anger is more acceptable when expressed in words, than in physical violence.
- *Make up*  Once the tantrum is over, let your child know that it is natural to feel angry and that you feel angry too sometimes. Make sure he knows that you still love him and that it's only his behaviour you don't like. Remember to congratulate him once he has regained control.

## Helping your child get on with others

Social skills and behaviour are important for your toddler's eventual emergence as an independent individual. These skills include the ability to meet, mix and communicate with other people; learning how to play, share, take turns with others and accept rules; mastering toilet training and adhering to general standards of cleanliness and eating in 'acceptable' ways. As your child acquires these social skills he will also gain independence and confidence and learn to value himself and others.

Learning how to make friends and get on with people is an essential part of growing up. A child who is friendly and well liked is more self confident, and has more fun and play opportunities.

Not every child is naturally confident and outgoing, however, and, like everything else, the ability to make friends and socialise has to be learnt. Young toddlers are 'egocentric', that is, the centre of their own worlds. Your toddler will be unable to understand the concept of sharing or the feelings of others, and playing with other children often leads to tears over a coveted toy.

As his self-knowledge grows, however, your child should begin to demonstrate that he is aware that what he feels is felt by others; this is known as empathy. He may even respond to another person's distress by becoming distressed himself. Empathy may encourage a child to become more generous and unselfish in play with others and is something you should try to help him to develop.

While aspects of your child's personality may have been apparent at birth (whether he cried a lot or was placid, for example) between the ages of two to three his true personality will become quite obvious.

While he is learning to master the various locomotive and manipulative skills, he will become aware of his ability to influence the actions of himself and others.

When he is unsuccessful in his attempts, he also will suffer from feelings of shame and failure. He must learn to handle both his successes and his failures in acceptable ways in order to become a well-balanced individual.

You can help your child to better integrate the different aspects of personality – activity, sociability and emotionality – by showing him how to tackle problems successfully, distracting him when he becomes frustrated, and by enabling him to construct a positive self-image through praise without ridiculing his fears.

## Promoting social skills

- Make sure your child is familiar with other children by going to places where there are other children present.
- Encourage loving behaviour towards other people, animals and dolls.
- Use public transport for outings and visit supermarkets and cafés where he will learn to queue and wait for his turn.
- If there is a dispute with another child over a toy, try not to intervene immediately, but stand by to sort out any fights and introduce the idea of sharing and taking turns.
- As soon as your child becomes old enough to understand, praise any attempts at sharing. At first he may share just to please you, rather than out of any sense of fairness. Suggest that each child take turns to play with a favourite toy. You could set an alarm clock to ring every five minutes or so.
- Teach him to say 'Please' and 'Thank you' at the appropriate times.

## Right and wrong

By the age of three you need to make sure that your toddler is aware of the difference between 'good' and 'bad' actions. Try and explain to your toddler in simple ways why you want him to do one thing and not another. Most children like to do what is right, although it doesn't always stop them being naughty, because naughtiness is a very good way of making you pay attention to them.

Rather than concentrating on the negative aspects of personality, the best tack is to use positive reinforcement as much as possible. Give praise when your toddler is careful in situations or with other people's feelings.

Many toddlers mix make-believe and reality or tell you things that are not strictly true. This is not lying but a natural part of behaviour at this age – some psychologists believe that children are only capable of lying after the age of four.

Some children constantly use the word 'No' even when they mean 'Yes' but this is simply their way of trying to assert authority.

## Problems with sociability

Some children have trouble focusing their attention on anything for any length of time, including playing with other children. Others go through a phase of temper tantrums, aggressiveness, extreme insecurity or rapid and frequent mood changes. Often this is a natural stage of development and you need not worry. However, if your child's 'bad' behaviour is prolonged or you are having trouble coping with it, ask your doctor or health visitor for some advice.

# Baby health guide

# Looking after your baby's health

Every year in the UK, women visit their doctors for health advice twice as often as men. It's the same old story about men not feeling the need to discuss their health issues, mental or physical, with anyone else. So it can be a shock for a new father when you have to take your child to the doctor's surgery. You probably won't be familiar with the procedures and etiquette of the waiting room or the consultation, and you may feel uncomfortable having to interpret your child's symptoms for the doctor.

With more dads taking an active role in the care of their children, and research showing how important their involvement is to child health and development, even the medical establishment is now recognising that fathers need more help from doctors. The American Academy of Pediatricians recently published guidance for its members, which went so far as to encourage them to change their practices and clinical style to better accommodate and involve fathers.

A good way to get to know the routine at your local surgery is to accompany your partner when your baby is called in for immunisations. Keeping up to date with all the regular vaccinations is vital for your child's health, but the injections can be a stressful experience for both baby and parents, so it makes sense to support your partner on the first visit, at least.

In the early years, it can feel like your child is constantly ill as she goes through the necessary chore of contracting almost every illness available in the local community while building up her immune system. This is exhausting for the whole family, especially when the bugs spread. And it's important to be aware of the extra strain on your partner when she's tending for a sick, demanding child. If your partner is breastfeeding, she may literally be drained of energy by your baby's attempts to gain comfort through continual suckling. While breastfed babies contract fewer infections than bottlefed babies, it may not seem like that at the time.

So, although it's your baby who is ill, it can be a very stressful time for mums and dads, making even minor illnesses much more difficult to handle. When you're up in the middle of the night trying to take a temperature or struggling to administer medicine to a hot, crying baby, it can be very difficult to know

## WE NEED TO TALK | ABOUT SICKNESS DAYS

When your partner and child are ill at the same time, and your partner is struggling to look after your child, this is when she really needs to feel your commitment to the family. But what if you are under pressure to perform at work and feel torn between the financial and emotional priorities? Your overriding loyalty must be to your family, but you have to be totally honest with your partner. Find out exactly what she feels is possible, or what favours you can call in from friends – you can be sure they will need help in return some day. The longer your partner struggles on, the longer the illness is likely to last. One day of rest may mean she will be better able to cope the following day. Everyone gets ill at some time and taking sick leave to care for your family should be no different than taking it when you are ill. As long as you can maintain your credibility at work, there should be no reason to feel guilty.

## When to see the doctor

Very young babies can become ill very quickly, so it is important to be aware of the symptoms that could indicate illness. If your baby develops any of the following symptoms, or appears unwell, urgent medical advice is required:

- Paleness or a bluish colour around the mouth and on the face.
- Fever with a temperature of 38°C (100.4°F) or more.

whether the problem is serious enough to call your doctor. You can always call the NHS helpline (111 in England) for telephone advice. Research has shown that when a child is feverish, parents tend to take inaccurate temperature readings and then give a child the wrong doses and types of medicine. The key to getting things right in these situations is to have all the necessary equipment and medicines on hand, and to keep a notepad to write down what you do, and what symptoms your child is showing, at what times. This helps you keep control of the situation, and provides a record to help the doctor with diagnosis should that be necessary. There are also some simple guidelines to follow, which can help (see box).

- Fever with a temperature of 38°C (100.4°F) or more.
- Refusing to be fed.
- Crying for unusually long periods.
- Blood-streaked stools.
- Vomiting that lasts for six hours or more, or is accompanied by fever and/or diarrhoea.
- Projectile vomiting.
- Diarrhoea – more than six to eight watery stools per day.
- Nose blocked by mucus, making it difficult for your baby to breathe while feeding.
- Redness or tenderness around the navel area.
- White patches in the mouth.
- Eyes are pink, bloodshot, have a sticky white discharge, or eyelashes that stick together.
- Baby's body becomes floppy or stiff.

## A VISIT TO THE DOCTOR

These tips should help you make the most of a visit to the surgery with your sick child, easing anxieties and giving your doctor the best chance of making an accurate diagnosis.

1 Write a list of your child's symptoms and when they occurred.

2 Write down any medicines you have given your child, including the time and dose.

3 Dress your child in clothing that is loose and easy to remove so that the doctor can examine her quickly and easily. Keep your child warm with a blanket or coat, if necessary.

4 If you have not been to the surgery recently, ask your partner what to do on arrival.

5 Take a drink for the baby and nappy changing gear, just as you would on any other trip.

# When your baby is ill

There are some basic skills you need to master so that you can comfort your sick baby and ensure that medicines are taken effectively. Small children can be very resistant to accepting what's good for them, and it can often require both parents working in tandem to get the medicine down. Don't expect to get it right first time and always have a cloth or tissues available to mop up the spills!

**Taking a temperature** A young baby's temperature should be taken under her arm. If you're using a digital thermometer, wipe under your baby's arm to remove any sweat, then place the bulb into the fold of her armpit and hold her arm against her side to keep it in place. Leave for three to four minutes or until the thermometer beeps. Normal body temperature is 37°C (98.6°F), contact your doctor if your baby's temperature is 38°C (100.4°F) or above. Always tell your doctor that you took the measurement under the arm (the axillary temperature), as this gives a slightly lower reading (about 0.7°C or 1°F).

With an older baby, a digital ear thermometer is worth the extra investment, because it takes an instant reading and remembers it.

Strip thermometers that can be held against the baby's forehead seem easier, but these are often unreliable and difficult to read.

**Giving medicine by oral syringe** This can be the only way to get medicine into a baby who is not used to a spoon, who is refusing to open her mouth or proving difficult to keep still. Most pharmacists can provide you with one. Cradle her in your arms and aim the tip of the syringe between her rear gums and cheek, avoiding the taste buds. Squirt the medicine slowly to avoid making her choke, and do not touch the back of the tongue with the syringe in case it causes her to gag.

**Giving medicine by dummy-style syringe** The nipple-shaped tip on this syringe allows your baby to suck while you express the medicine. Hold your baby in your lap, supporting her head in the crook of your arm. Put the tip of the syringe in her mouth, as you would with a bottle, and slowly press the plunger.

**Administering eye drops** This can be a tricky operation and it may be wise to swaddle your baby to prevent her wriggling. Lay her on her back and tilt her head to one side, with the affected eye nearest your leg. Taking care not to touch the eye with the dropper, pull down her lower eyelid and squeeze the drops into the eye. You may need help to hold her head steady.

**Administering ear drops** Lay your baby on her side with the affected ear facing upwards. The medicine needs to be dropped down into the ear canal, so straighten the canal by gently pulling back the earlobe. Bring the dropper close to her ear to ensure you hit the target, and hold her steady while the drops sink in, using cotton wool to soak up any leaks.

**Sponging your baby** Bringing down your baby's high temperature will comfort her and help her feel less irritable. Wrap her in a towel and sit her on your lap. Gently wipe her down with a sponge soaked in water that has been boiled and then cooled to a lukewarm temperature.

# Caring for some common conditions

## Colds

Colds are caused by different viruses and your child is likely to have about eight colds a year until age 12, while his immunity builds up. A cough may develop with a cold but if your child is eating and breathing normally and there is no wheezing, usually it is nothing to worry about. Although colds and coughs can cause discomfort they rarely need treatment; antibiotics will not help unless a secondary bacterial infection develops.

Apply petroleum jelly around your child's nose to stop it becoming sore. Keep your child cool and give him plenty of fluids. Avoid overusing cough mixture – a warm drink of lemon and honey can be just as soothing.

Seek medical advice if your child is wheezing or has difficulty breathing, has a temperature of more than 38°C (100.4°F), seems to be in pain when coughing, or the cough continues for a long time.

## Croup

A respiratory infection of the larynx or voice box, croup is caused by a virus or by bacteria. Characterised by a harsh or barking cough, a runny nose, hoarseness, noisy breathing and fever, it is common in children up to the age of four. Most cases of croup are mild and do not last long. but it can be very alarming. Stay calm or you may frighten your child. Reassure him and sit him up. Create a steamy atmosphere to help breathing. For example, sit in the bathroom and run the hot taps, use a humidifier, put wet towels over a warm radiator or boil a kettle – keep your child well away from the steam to avoid scalding. Keep the door and windows closed and encourage your child to breathe in and out. Give warm drinks and treat the fever with the recommended dose of infant paracetamol.

However, seek medical advice or take your child to hospital if he becomes distressed, or has difficulty in breathing or swallowing, turns blue, or there is indrawing of the ribs or below the ribs, when breathing.

## Fever

If your baby has skin that is warm to the touch, is reluctant to feed, is lethargic or shows signs of a possible infection, such as a cold, check whether your baby has a fever. A temperature of more than 38°C (100.4°F) is a fever; in very young babies the temperature can rise very quickly.

There are several reasons why a baby may develop a fever right after birth. His mother may have an infection that has been passed on to him, for example. Even if the mother has a normal temperature, an infection can cause a fever in her baby. Less likely, a raised temperature can be related to the baby's environment: if the delivery room or nursery is too hot, a baby's temperature may increase.

No matter what the cause, a raised temperature in a new or very young baby should never be ignored; it may be the first indication of a more serious problem. In a new baby it usually indicates an infection of some kind. He may have caught a bacterial infection during birth or may have become infected with a cold virus from a visitor. Either way, you should call your doctor as treatment may be required.

What's particularly important when your child has a fever is to make a note of his temperature each time you take it, so that you can keep track of any changes. Bear in mind that there are several things you can do to reduce your baby's temperature before resorting to medicine. Look at his immediate environment and ask yourself: 'What is he wearing; can any of these clothes can be removed? Is the room too hot, and can I make it cooler? Is he lying on a thick blanket that reflects heat, and if so, can it be removed? Am I holding him so close that my own body heat is pushing up his temperature; shall I lay him down? When did he last have a cool drink; shall I give him some water?' These measures should help as his body fights off the infection. Don't let him become too hot as this can trigger febrile seizures, overleaf.

To reduce the fever give your child the recommended dose of infant paracetamol or infant ibuprofen. Never give it to a baby under three months unless your doctor recommends it. Do not give your child both paracetamol and ibuprofen unless advised to by your doctor. Never give aspirin to a child under the age of 12 as there is a small risk of a condition called Reyes syndrome. Offer him plenty of cool drinks.

### Febrile seizures

If your child's temperature rises too far above normal, this may result in a febrile seizure. Your child suddenly becomes rigid, stares without blinking, or his limbs start to twitch or jerk. He may become blue and lose consciousness for a few minutes. While frightening, febrile seizures are quite common, especially in children between six months and three years of age, and are due to a child's temperature-lowering mechanism in the brain being too immature to cope.

If your child has a seizure, try not to panic. Place pillows or soft padding around the child and/or move any objects that could be harmful out of the way; do not put anything in the mouth and never try to restrain him. Remove any bedding and undress your baby down to his nappy – you may have to wait until the seizures stop; most seizures cease after three minutes. Fan him and open a window if necessary, but don't let him get too cold. Do not sponge

him with water in your efforts to reduce his temperature. When the seizures stop, lay him on his side, with his head tilted back slightly, so that the airway is clear. Stay with your child. Reassure him and call your doctor or an ambulance. Once his temperature is lowered, cover him lightly in a cotton sheet. Keep checking his temperature. If his temperature begins to rise again while you are waiting for the doctor, repeat the cooling measures.

### Meningitis

This is an inflammation of the membranes that line the brain and spinal cord. It's usually caused by a viral or bacterial infection. Viral meningitis may be caused by a number of different viruses, and is commonly mild, with no long-term side effects. Very occasionally it can be severe and cause serious problems.

With a newborn, bacterial meningitis is usually caused by Group B streptococcus. In babies over three months, the three most common forms of meningitis are: haemophilus influenzae Type B (Hib); meningococcus Groups A, B and C. Group B is the most common, but Group C is the most severe and requires immediate hospital treatment, as it can be fatal if not treated early.

If you suspect meningitis, call an ambulance without delay or take your baby to the hospital for urgent evaluation. Meningitis may be hard to diagnose, so your healthcare provider may perform a

lumbar puncture to confirm any diagnosis. Antibiotics will be given if bacterial meningitis is suspected. A hearing test may be carried out after four weeks, as deafness is the most common side effect of bacterial meningitis. If the infection is viral, your baby should recover within a few days.

### Earache

A pain in the ear may be caused by an infection in the middle ear (otitis media), by another infection such as measles or mumps, or even toothache. Symptoms include fever, severe pain, general malaise and vomiting. If the ear drum

---

### SIGNS OF MENINGITIS
- High-pitched crying
- Drowsiness or lethargy
- Bulging fontanelle (soft spot) on the top of a baby's head
- Vomiting
- Refusal to feed
- Pale skin and cold limbs
- Sensitivity to light
- Fever and a blank, staring expression
- Stiffness of the neck
- Difficulty breathing
- A convulsion with stiffened body and shaking
- Reddish-purple spots that don't go away if pressed with a glass – these are small bruises under the skin

---

## FIRST AID FOR CHOKING

Babies under a year old usually choke because they have breathed in a foreign object, which can lodge at the back of the throat and cause muscle spasm. This may block the airway and must be removed immediately. If you suspect your baby is choking but he can still cry and cough, allow him to continue coughing. Watch carefully but do not pat his back or give water.

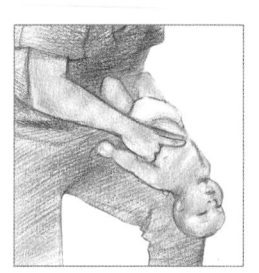

**If he cannot cry, cough or breathe,** lay him face down along your forearm or lap, supporting his head with your hand. With the heel of your other hand, strike your baby between the shoulder blades up to five times. Each strike should be a separate attempt to dislodge the object. Check the mouth. Remove any obvious obstructions, but do not do sweep your fingers in his mouth.

**If your baby is still choking,** carefully turn him over, check his mouth again. If he is still not breathing, place two or three fingers on the lower part of the breastbone and press inwards and downwards towards his head (chest thrust). Each thrust should be a separate attempt to dislodge the object.
Give up to five chest thrusts and check the mouth again. If the obstruction is still not cleared, repeat three cycles of five back blows, five chest thrusts, and mouth checks, then dial 999 (or 112) for an ambulance. Continue as above until help arrives.

**If your baby loses consciousness and you don't know if he's breathing,** place him on his back on a firm surface, tilting his head back slightly. Look along his chest, feel for breaths against your ear and listen for breathing sounds for up to 10 seconds. If there is no sign of breathing, get someone to call for help and begin cardiopulmonary resuscitation or **CPR** (see page 126) – this is a combination of rescue breaths and chest compressions.

---

bursts, yellow or green pus or blood may be seen in the ear or on the pillow.

If your child has earache but is otherwise well, give the recommended dose of infant paracetamol or ibuprofen for 12–24 hours. Do not put any oil or eardrops into your child's ear. Hold a covered hot water bottle or a heat pad against your child's ear to relieve pain. If your child

continues to be uncomfortable, or appears to have an infection, consult your doctor. He may either prescribe antibiotics or suggest pain relief and decongestant nose drops. After an ear infection a child may have a hearing problem for up to six weeks.

### Diarrhoea

Usually caused by the rotovirus infection, diarrhoea is characterised

by frequent, loose, watery, foul-smelling stools, which may contain mucus and may be brown, yellow or green. Toddlers may also get a condition called toddler diarrhoea where bouts of passing very loose stools, which may contain bits of undigested food, occur for no apparent reason.

If the diarrhoea is very watery or contains blood, it continues for more than 48 hours, your child is

## (CPR) CARDIOPULMONARY RESUSCITATION FOR BABIES UNDER ONE YEAR

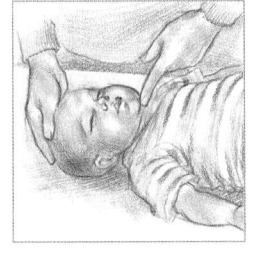

1   Lay your baby down on a firm flat surface such as the floor or a table, then gently tilt his head back with one hand, and lift his chin with the other to open his airway. It's important not to tilt his head back too far as this could kink his airway. Put your ear to his mouth and nose, and look, listen and feel for breathing. If you are on your own give CPR for one minute before you call an ambulance.

2   If your baby is not breathing, begin Rescue Breaths. Ensure the airway is open, take a normal breath, then seal your lips around his mouth over his nose and lips. Blow gently into the mouth until you see the chest rise. Remove your mouth and repeat to give FIVE breaths.

3   Then give 30 chest compressions. Place two fingers of your lower hand on the centre of the baby's chest. Press down sharply about one-third of the depth of the chest. Release the pressure and let the chest come back up, but don't move your fingers. Press 30 times at a rate of 100 per minute.

4   After 30 compressions, give TWO further Rescue Breaths. Continue with a sequence of 30 compressions followed by TWO Rescue Breaths without stopping until the baby shows signs of recovery (begins coughing, and breathing normally) or emergency help arrives.

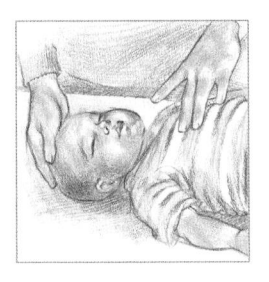

5   If the baby recovers but remains unconscious, hold him with his head down in the recovery position.

also vomiting, or has signs of dehydration (dry skin or mouth, sunken eyes, does not pass water for six to eight hours, or is listless), contact your doctor immediately.

Give your child plenty of clear fluids or an oral electrolyte fluid. Let him eat if he wants to but avoid too much milk or fruit.

### Chickenpox

A common and mild viral infection, which most children have had by the age of 10, the virus is easily spread by airborne droplets. In rare cases it can lead to encephalitis.

Spots appear mainly in crops over three to four days. These change to blisters and crust over. Your child will have a slight fever and appears unwell and may have a headache.

To soothe the itching, apply calamine lotion, or give the child a tepid bath with a cup of bicarbonate of soda or oatmeal added. Discourage scratching as it can cause scarring. For a fever, give the recommended dose of paracetamol and plenty to drink. Never give aspirin, see page 124. Contact your doctor; your doctor may prescribe antiseptic cream.

Try to keep your child away from anyone who is pregnant as contacting chickenpox in pregnancy may cause serious problems for the mother and baby. If your child was with anyone pregnant just before he became unwell, tell the woman to see her doctor.

### Fifth Disease

A fairly common but mild viral infection, usually occurring in the spring. The major symptom is a slap mark on cheek, which lasts one to two days. Over the next two to three days, a lacy red rash

appears on the body. It may come and go for up to two weeks. There may be fever and nasal discharge.

Treat the fever by keeping your child cool and give him plenty to drink (see page 124). The child is not contagious once the rash appears so does not need to be kept away from others. The rash generally causes no discomfort and goes away eventually without treatment. There are no complications.

## German measles (rubella)

This is a viral disease, which is usually mild in children but can be serious for adults, therefore it is best to be exposed to it as a child. Rubella can be prevented by immunisation.

It may start like a cold but spots appear on the face, and spread to the rest of the body. The rash usually only lasts for a few days. Your child will usually feel fine but he may have a slight fever and enlarged lymph nodes at the back of his neck on the lower part of the skull. Give him plenty to drink. Keep the child away from pregnant women – if a pregnant woman catches rubella during the first four months of pregnancy, there is a serious risk of damage to her baby.

## Whooping cough

This is a very distressing disease and can be dangerous in young children, but it can be prevented by immunisation. Complications include pneumonia, convulsions, ear infections, brain damage and death. Keep a child with whooping cough away from non-immunised babies.

Whooping cough starts with a cold and cough but the cough gradually gets worse and changes so that several bouts occur in succession. These are exhausting for your child who may find it difficult to breathe and may vomit or choke. The coughing usually, but not always, ends with a 'whoop' as the child gasps for breath. It may last for several weeks.

Call your doctor. Antibiotics will be needed, and in severe cases, hospitalisation. Keep your child cool. Give drinks and offer food immediately after a coughing bout. If your child is having a severe bout of coughing, place him on your knee, lean him forward and gently pat and rub his back to help loosen the mucus.

## Impetigo

This common bacterial skin infection in children usually occurs around the nose and mouth. It spreads rapidly, especially in warm weather. Complications can include swelling of lymph nodes, septicaemia or kidney inflammation.

Spots form blisters filled with yellow sticky fluid which oozes from the skin. The fluid dries to form honey-coloured crusts on the skin.

Consult your doctor immediately because impetigo spreads rapidly if left untreated. Topical antibiotics, covered by dressings, and sometimes oral antibiotics will be needed. Wash away crusted areas with warm water; pat dry with paper towels. Keep your child's flannel, towels and bedlinen separate from the rest of the family. Keep your child away from other children until he is fully recovered.

## Infantile eczema

Also known as atopic dermatitis, this is the most common form of eczema in babies under 12 months. Eczema is an allergic condition related to asthma and hay fever. It can be inherited but also can exist in isolation. It commonly appears on the face and scalp or behind the ears. Your baby may only have a few patches of dry skin; but if the eczema is severe, your baby's skin may become sore, inflamed and weepy. This is unbearably itchy, so your baby will scratch continuously, leaving his skin open to infection.

Though it can only be managed, not cured, most children do grow out of atopic eczema. It is important to maintain a strict skin-care regime under medical supervision. Emollients will prevent your baby's skin from getting too dry and itchy. Steroid creams can reduce inflammation, but are generally only used if your baby's eczema hasn't responded to emollients. Antibiotics may be prescribed to clear up infection in severe cases.

Wearing mitts will help to stop a baby scratching. Breastfeeding for the first six months may give some protection against allergens.

# Index

**Acknowledgements**
Products supplied by Mothercare.
All products available at
www.mothercare.com

**Picture Credits**
P 2/3 Camera Press/Eltern: P 7 Terry
Allen/Photolibrary Group: P 9
Camera Press/Eltern: P 12
Photolibrary Group: P 16,19, 21, 44
Getty Images: P 51 Camera
Press/Eltern: P 52 Getty Images
P 56 Camera Press/Richard
Stonehouse: P 57
www.bloomingmarvellous.co.uk:
P 58t, b, 68, 70, 82, 84, 87, 88t, 92/3
Getty Images: P 97 Camera
Press/Richard Stonehouse: P 102
Camera Press/Images 24: P 108
Camera Press/Richard Stonehouse:
P 113, 121 Getty Images
Front jacket Getty Images